OREGON

Preserving the Spirit and Beauty of Our Land

Text by Tim Palmer
Photography by Terry Donnelly and Mary Liz Austin
Foreword by John Daniel

Voyageur Press

Edited by Margret Aldrich
Designed by Andrea Rud
Printed in China

03 04 05 06 07   5 4 3 2 1

Library of Congress Cataloging-in-Publication Data
Palmer, Tim, 1948–
  Oregon : preserving the spirit and beauty of our land / text by Tim Palmer ; photography by Terry Donnelly and Mary Liz Austin ; foreword by John Daniel.
    p. cm.
Includes bibliographical references and index.
  ISBN 0-89658-532-8 (hardcover)
  1. Oregon—Pictorial works. 2. Natural history—Oregon—Pictorial works. 3. Oregon—Description and travel. 4. Natural history—Oregon.
I. Donnelly, Terry, 1949– II. Austin, Mary Liz. III. Title.
  F877.P28 2003
  917.9504'44—dc21
                    2003008801

Distributed in Canada by Raincoast Books,
9050 Shaughnessy Street, Vancouver, B.C. V6P 6E5

Published by Voyageur Press, Inc.
123 North Second Street, P.O. Box 338, Stillwater, MN 55082 U.S.A.
651-430-2210, fax 651-430-2211
books@voyageurpress.com
www.voyageurpress.com

Educators, fundraisers, premium and gift buyers, publicists, and marketing managers: Looking for creative products and new sales ideas? Voyageur Press books are available at special discounts when purchased in quantities, and special editions can be created to your specifications. For details contact the marketing department at 800-888-9653.

Fine art prints of the images that appear in this book can be ordered through the photographers' website at www.donnelly-austin.com.

ON PAGE 1: MORNING SUNLIGHT SHINES GOLDEN ON THE FACE OF THREE FINGERED JACK IN THE MOUNT JEFFERSON WILDERNESS.

ON PAGE 2: LOWER TABLE ROCK, BORDERING THE ROGUE VALLEY, IS A VITAL REFUGE PROTECTED BY THE OREGON NATURE CONSERVANCY.

ON PAGE 3: SILVER FALLS IS AMONG THE MANY PARKS THAT MAKE OREGON'S STATE PARK SYSTEM ONE OF THE FINEST IN AMERICA.

ON PAGE 4: THE SOUTH SISTER, ONE OF THE QUEEN PEAKS OF THE OREGON CASCADES, REFLECTS IN THE CALM WATERS OF SPARKS LAKE.

ON PAGE 5: RED ALDERS HAVE TAKEN OVER IN MANY PLACES WHERE OLD-GROWTH CONIFERS WERE CLEAR-CUT IN THE SIUSLAW NATIONAL FOREST.

ON PAGE 6: YELLOW BEE-PLANT AND JOHN DAY CHAENACTIS COLOR THE PAINTED HILLS IN THE JOHN DAY FOSSIL BEDS NATIONAL MONUMENT.

ON PAGE 7: THIS MARSH IN BLASKETT SLOUGH NATIONAL WILDLIFE REFUGE IS A REMNANT OF RICH WETLAND COMPLEXES LIKE THOSE THAT ONCE NOURISHED THE WILLAMETTE RIVER AND ABSORBED ITS HIGH RUNOFF, MAKING FLOODS LESS SEVERE DOWNSTREAM.

ON PAGE 8: EUROPEAN BEACHGRASS INVADES THE SAND DUNES AND DISPLACES NATIVE PLANTLIFE AT THE MOUTH OF THE SIXES RIVER IN CAPE BLANCO STATE PARK.

ON PAGE 9: FOG SHROUDS THE COQUILLE RIVER LIGHTHOUSE AT BULLARDS BEACH STATE PARK IN BANDON.

ON PAGE 10: THE WALLOWA MOUNTAINS STRETCH ACROSS THE HORIZON OF THE ZUMWALT PRAIRIE.

ON PAGE 11: CRATER LAKE, OREGON'S ONLY NATIONAL PARK, SHINES IN THE MOONLIGHT BENEATH MOUNT SCOTT.

ON PAGE 12: MIDDLE NORTH FORK FALLS HIGHLIGHTS THE SPRINGTIME IN SILVER FALLS STATE PARK EAST OF SALEM.

DEDICATION

This collection of words and images, inspired by the natural landscape, is dedicated to the people who have protected the wild places we cherish.

ACKNOWLEDGMENTS

I could never offer too many thanks to my wife, Ann Vileisis, for her spirited support as I wrote the text to this book, for her sharp insight, editing skills, and full partnership in my life here in Oregon.

Next to her, I most want to thank Terry Donnelly and Mary Liz Austin for inviting me to join them in this joint effort—for the opportunity and honor to write alongside their superb photographs.

Jim Britell, an extraordinary man who did much to protect the forests of the southern coast, made it both possible and irresistible for Ann and me to live here and to truly adopt this magnificent place as the finest home we can imagine. Both the uncut beauty of Bald Mountain—rising so elegantly between the Pacific and the Elk River—and a soulful part of this book stand as a tribute to this man's dedication and vision.

Two great conservationists from decades ago—Bob Potter and Bob Peirce—first introduced me to Oregon's rivers. In the following generation, Don Elder of River Network in Portland has always inspired me and a multitude of other people with his leadership. Stephen Anderson of The Oregon Nature Conservancy graciously checked my work for errors and supplied me with good information about this place that he has written so much and so well about himself.

Thanks to John Daniel for the foreword to this book and for all the excellent writing he does; Oregon could have no better spokesman in the literary world. Finally, Margret Aldrich is so competent, smart, and dedicated—it has been a pleasure to have her as my editor.

—Tim Palmer

We are greatly indebted to Steven Anderson and the Oregon Nature Conservancy for providing and encouraging access to the most incredible places in Oregon. The impressions of awe left by the time we spent on the Zumwalt Prairie will long remain with us.

We would like to acknowledge Larry Geddis and Bruce Jackson, two of Oregon's finest landscape photographers, for their selfless advice on the unique beautiful locations and fickle weather conditions of their home state.

Muchas gracias to John Botkin and the staff wizards of Photo Craft Lab in Boulder, Colorado, for quick and reliable service.

Recognition is also due to our office staff: Ruth Anderson, Marie Harrington, and Margie Morgan. We owe them countless thanks for all the extra effort required at home while we are on the road.

—Terry Donnelly and Mary Liz Austin

CONTENTS

FOREWORD

By John Daniel

Longtime Oregon resident John Daniel is the author of six books of poetry, essays, and memoir. He has been the recipient of a Wallace Stegner fellowship at Stanford University, the John Burroughs Outstanding Nature Essay Award, and a fellowship from the National Endowment for the Arts. Two of his books, *The Trail Home* and *Looking After: A Son's Memoir*, have won the Oregon Book Award for literary nonfiction.

Back in the 1950s and 60s, when I was growing up in the suburbs of Washington, D.C., the name "Oregon" had an uncanny allure. I used to speak the word aloud sometimes as I tramped the Blue Ridge woods near my family's weekend cabin in northern Virginia. What I said, no doubt, was "ARE-uh-GAHN," a pronunciation that now makes me cringe, but the attraction to a place I'd never seen was real and insistent. Oregon was the land where Lewis and Clark had gone, trading with Indians as they canoed down a river many times longer and broader than D.C.'s polluted Potomac. It was the land where mountains were higher and trees were taller and fish were bigger than any I knew, the land where a different ocean pounded a coast that was nothing like, I was sure, the crowded sand beaches of Delaware. Oregon was the land where I wanted to be.

Now, having lived in the state for the better part of four decades, I've lost the rapture of my puppy love from afar, but my feeling for the Oregon land has only grown as I've become more familiar with it. "We're lucky to live here," I say to my wife, or she says to me, many times a year. I fly the state flag off the stern of our house, where its gold beaver on a blue background snaps crisply in the afternoon wind that stirs the Douglas firs and wild hazelnuts in summer, thus acting out what is surely the loveliest of all state mottoes: "She Flies with Her Own Wings."

We Oregonians are lucky, all right. In our three-hundred-by-four-hundred-mile state, we've got a long and varied seashore as beautiful as any in the world; wet, rainforested rumples of coastal mountains; one great valley of rich farmland and several smaller ones; a range of young and boisterous volcanic peaks; expanses of sage-and-juniper steppe broken by fault-block mountains; rocky desert folded into hills and inscribed with deeply worn canyons; a half-state membership in one of the great river systems in western North America; scores of smaller drainages of greatly diverse character; a smattering of lakes, including the deepest and bluest lake in the United States; and even a granitic outlier of the Rocky Mountains, which probably wandered into northeastern Oregon because it couldn't stand to be left out of a landscape so vibrantly diverse.

We don't like it our way, we like it all ways, and the variegated splendor of our state is well represented in Terry Donnelly's and Mary Liz Austin's photographs. From the sea stacks of Bandon to the rolling Cascades to the shining shoulders of Eagle Cap, from the Columbia Gorge to the aspened canyons of Steens Mountain to the stark yellow beauty of Leslie Gulch, from old-growth cedars to Oregon white oaks to the timberline's hard-working whitebark pines—from bear grass to rabbit brush, sword ferns to sage, there's a wild place shown here for every spirit, for every mood that wants out of town.

Tim Palmer, your knowledgeable guide, followed his own Oregon Trail from the East and fell into the same kind of love that I did. He will take you across the state and show you around, and along the way he will answer questions you might not have thought to ask. Why does the coast have summer fog? How do various species of trees deal with the burden of snow? How do exotic annual grasses beat out the native bunchgrasses? How many waves hit Ecola State Park in a day? Which Cascade volcanoes are likeliest to blow?

He will also ask you to think about what you do not see in these photographs—the ways we have taxed and troubled the Oregon land, both outside and within the protected reserves that are the sources of most of these images. We are lucky to live among such riches. It will take more than luck—it will take humility, wisdom, and caring action—to maintain this wealth that we have inherited and that our descendants deserve to inherit from us.

John Daniel

EVENING LIGHT WARMS THE SLOPES OF HART MOUNTAIN IN SOUTH-CENTRAL OREGON.

A PLACE OF EXTRAVAGANT BEAUTY

People throughout history have approached the land of Oregon with great anticipation. The first Americans no doubt came into this region with fascination and reverence for the local natural wealth. Whether migrating along the coast in dugout canoes or working their way down the Columbia River from the glacier-free corridor of the interior West, the Indians surely recognized a land of plenty, alive with salmon, elk, berries, cedar for their boats and lodges, and all the necessary staples of life.

A dozen millennia later, in 1805, the primary goal of Lewis and Clark's expedition was to reach the coast of Oregon, and after these most celebrated of American explorers reported back about rivers semi-solid with fish, trees of mind-boggling girth, and a winter of soaking dampness beyond belief, the myths of this little-known frontier began to grow. Some of those myths were true. Some have persisted whether true or not. Some have died, allowing others to rise and take the place of the old. Amazingly elusive, a true understanding of this land is something people have always had to struggle to achieve.

In the wake of Lewis and Clark, the Oregon Trail drew colonizing Americans by the thousands. Here lay the original "promised land" of the West, and the push to settle came even before the Gold Rush to California. Having never seen so much as a photo, and not really knowing what to expect, wagon train after wagon train of Americans pinned high hopes on a place they had heard would fulfill their dreams. Few, however, anticipated such a blistering desert, such a fungus-rotting rainforest, such intimidating barriers of lava and impenetrable drifts of snow blowing down from glacial heights. And certainly nobody from Massachusetts or Pennsylvania or Missouri—as beautiful as those places are—could have anticipated the beauty that is simply extravagant here in the Pacific Northwest. The real Oregon was something no one had imagined very well.

Skipping ahead a century or so to when I grew up in the 1950s, the Beaver State had a reputation as a logger's paradise, and indeed it was. Vast reaches of clear-grained forest still lay uncut. As a kid, I wanted to go to Oregon and be a lumberjack. With my dad's ax, I practiced in the woods out back. But seeing something else in the great northwestern forests—seeing the remarkable diversity of life and the abundance of captivating scenes of fecundity—a new breed of enthusiast in the 1970s adopted the state as "ecotopia." These people thought of Oregon as a place where we might all live in balance with nature and celebrate some of the remaining wildness rather than always eliminate it.

As the twenty-first century begins, Oregon still appeals because of its nature and beauty, but now it has also become a magnet for greater numbers of people than ever before—far greater. Newcomers seek the quality of life that has eluded them or been lost with rapid

WILDFLOWERS GRACE THE ROLLING HILLS OF ZUMWALT PRAIRIE.

growth of cities and states elsewhere. Today's pioneers continue to follow the Oregon Trail—many Oregon trails—and everybody harbors high expectations for this extraordinary place.

It's not one place, but many: the Pacific edge an incomparable meeting of rock and sea, the coastal mountains an intricate mosaic of forests scribed by exquisite small streams, the Columbia River a stunning corridor between erupted volcanoes at the state's northern boundary. The Cascade Mountains rise as a strato-volcanic backbone ribbed by deep forests of fabulous life and complexity. The central and eastern portions of the state—beyond the blessing of rainfall that plentifully greens the more stereotypical Oregon—offer a land of ponderosa pine, golden grassy range, and glowing desert intrigue.

With all this and more, Oregon is emblematic of the American West. A semi-arid interior is followed by brilliant shining mountains, fertile valleys, and the Pacific coast. But Oregon is also unique with the massif of Steens Mountain jutting up from alkali plains, with the snow-cone profile of Mount Hood. Crater Lake is America's deepest and bluest lake. The Columbia is America's fourth-largest river and the largest in the West, its gorge utterly massive (only the Mississippi, St. Lawrence, and Ohio Rivers are larger). The forests of the western Cascades and coastal mountains rate among the greatest coniferous woodlands worldwide, the remaining old-growth a showcase of giant trees found only in the temperate Northwest. The changing profiles of forest and rock and water cause me to reflect on both permanence and transience. The vastness of the sea meeting the hard face of the continent causes me to consider unlimited opportunities but also undeniable limits here where the land emphatically ends.

Any view here reveals the powerful dictates of nature: a dramatic climate that governs everything it touches, vivid landforms shaped by the most primal geologic force, lush and varied plant life forming the building blocks of habitat for all creatures, and people who live in harmony with their world but also in devastating conflict with the very forces that make life itself possible.

From prehistoric times until today, people have come to Oregon because the land offers a mighty promise: we can live well among superlative natural wealth and beauty. But now, the wealth has been

VOLCANIC ROCKS BALANCE ABOVE THE METOLIUS RIVER CANYON.

divided again and again—the forests, fisheries, and rangelands have been consumed ever more quickly since that first wagon train forded the Snake River and peeked up from behind the Blue Mountains. Yet much of value still remains, and to know it better—to understand it and live in lasting balance with it—we have to look carefully, our thoughts genuinely receptive to all that's around us, our eyes wide open. This is important because most of us only learn to know and appreciate what we can see. If something is out-of-sight, then it's out-of-mind as well. And once that happens, whatever was special and precious becomes forgotten and lost.

Though their anticipation ran high, none of the early settlers knew what they would see when they arrived here, and neither do the modern pioneers. For that matter, even children growing up in this rapidly changing place may be unaware of their state's natural heritage. But by immersing ourselves in this book's photos, we can grasp some idea of the beauty and complexity that remains in the world around us. By paging through these colorful and captivating pictures of coast and gorge, mountain and plain, it's not so difficult to imagine a spirit of the land that has moved people so powerfully to appreciate the true nature of Oregon.

Old-growth forests, including this grove of ponderosa pines along the Metolius River,
are among the great natural masterpieces of the Oregon landscape.

CHAPTER 1

THE PACIFIC EDGE

Beginning with the Power of the Sea

I have a favorite beach in Oregon. I'm not going to say where it is, because people like to find their own favorite places. But mine is a mile-long crescent of sand edged by unclimbable cliffs, with a steep and formidable mountain anchoring one end and a craggy rock outcrop guarding the other.

It takes some effort to get to this place. I bushwhack and test my tolerance to poison oak, then scramble down a crumbly chute. But once I'm there, the rest of the world disappears. It's just me and the ocean and the outermost edge of Oregon.

Coyotes jog the sands, and seals bob as close to me as they can float. Those round-headed, bristly whiskered pinnipeds make eye contact as if we had once met—as if we had met and then separated—long ago. When I'm lucky, I see whales spouting offshore. They surface, then dive, suddenly here, then suddenly gone, and the disappearance of such an enormous creature suggests that much might lie hidden in other places as well.

There on my beach, as I sit and lean back against the first rock that guards the rest of America, I take all this in with a deep sense of appreciation. I breathe contentedly, knowing that a wild earth still has much to offer to any man or woman who is open to it. This place offers beauty and peace, adventure and solitude. And it offers something indefinably more than that. There's a spirit to it all. Surely I'm not the only one who feels this in my bones and in my heart whenever I pause where the ocean meets the shore.

Standing there on wet sand, with 6,000 miles of water ahead of me and 3,000 miles of land behind, I hate to leave such a pivotal position. I hate to change anything in the magisterial but delicate balance I feel deep inside. I've stayed until sunset, the golden light in heavenly rays beaming through offshore fog, followed by stars that fall like glitter into the darkening wilderness of sky.

SUNSET FADES TO AFTERGLOW AT THREE ARCH ROCKS AND OCEANSIDE BEACH NEAR TILLAMOOK.

SEA STACKS

Far more accessible than my favorite beach and just as alluring, the sea stacks at Bandon are like a tiny archipelago showing just how enchanted the coast of Oregon can be. You can stroll on the sand in a sculpture garden of rocky buttes, isolated obelisks, and staunchly capped domes that reflect the supreme forces at play here, where North America comes to a dramatic end, where the Pacific stages its mysterious beginnings.

The Oregon shore—290 miles as the crow flies or 367 miles the way you'd bike or drive—ranks as one of America's most spectacular coastlines. In my opinion it's tops, at least in the lower forty-eight states, though you have to get away from the main road and away from the sprawl oozing out of the beach towns to fully discover the magic of the place.

A steep, rocky rise of capes, headlands, and cliffs covers half the coastal distance. From south to north, Cape Ferrello, Sebastian, Blanco, Arago, Falcon, and a dozen others confront the sea as the leading edge of land, out there breaking the waves for the rest of the continent. Smooth swaths of beach and dunes cover the other half. In some places the beach is so broad and so flat that you can wander freeform. You can waltz in a spacious outdoor ballroom, the surf tuned-up like a whole philharmonic—strings, brass, and timpani.

More than anyplace else, this edge shows the dynamism of nature: waves that have gained strength since leaving the Gulf of Alaska wash against a shoreline formed by tremendous seismic forces. Winter storms drench mossy forests. In the same tilt of an ear it's possible to hear the bugling of elk and the barking of sea lions. Whales spout and blow, some staying all summer, others pausing exactly midway on their 12,000-mile trip from the winter bays of Baja to the plankton soup of the Bering Sea—the longest mammal migration on earth. Their backs and tails break the surface and then quickly return to the deep, a place that's imponderable to us but home to them.

Here at the seacoast, our tour of Oregon begins.

OFFSHORE ROCKS AT BANDON RISE LIKE MONUMENTS
IN AN OVERPOWERING SEA.

FALSE LILY-OF-THE-VALLEY

Winter storms pummel the Oregon coast with 80 to 200 inches of rain a year. They call it winter, but it's really the whole time from November through April. A taxonomist's array of native plants thrives with this hearty gift of nourishment. The false lily-of-the-valley, also called May lily, carpets forest floors and blankets the tops of nurse logs—the old fallen and decaying giants that offer a welcoming habitat for young plants. Though tasteless to us, the berries of this lily make a meal for small mammals.

Like much of the groundcover within the deep shade of evergreen forests, the lily leaves are flattened to the sky, exposing their full surface upward in order to harvest the most light possible in their cloudy, tree-shaded niche. Often growing in community with the dark-berried shrub called salal, and beneath protective arms of the mighty Sitka spruce, a simple glade of lilies can remind us how rich the native land of Oregon can be.

ECOLA STATE PARK

Eight thousand waves a day pound the shore, marching in from the northwest in summer and the southwest in winter. Swelling under the push of prevailing winds, the waves build in size and momentum and then break into spumy white foam when they approach the shallows. With a fetch running thousands of miles out to sea, big swells delight an athletic cast of surfers and also entertain people who simply come to watch waves be waves—rolling, building, peaking, breaking, sudsing, crashing, rebounding, never ending and always moving, forever changing. During winter storms at the headlands, saltwater explodes a hundred feet high on the rocks. Ten stories up, you can get wet even when it's not raining, and you lick salt from your lips.

FALSE LILY-OF-THE-VALLEY GROW THICKLY IN THE SHADE OF A SITKA SPRUCE FOREST ALONG THE COAST.

All along the Oregon coast the wind that causes these waves is a presence with which to reckon. As I stand and watch, it drifts the sand, which moves along the ground like a visible ghost showing exactly where the wind blows. It's like *seeing* the air.

There is no better place than Ecola State Park to enjoy this grand show of earthly forces converging on the Oregon coast.

STORM CLOUDS ROLL IN FROM THE SEA AT ECOLA STATE PARK ON OREGON'S NORTH COAST.

CASCADE HEAD

The sand of Oregon's beaches is brought to sea by Coast Range streams such as the Salmon River where it empties into the Pacific. These foxglove are an exotic species, introduced from Europe and highly poisonous. With native grasses and forbs, they bloom on the southern flank of Cascade Head, the highest point rising directly up from the Oregon shore, protected by both Nature Conservancy and Forest Service preserves. Exotic plants are being removed here to make room for the re-colonization of native vegetation.

ABOVE: THE TRUNK OF AN OLD-GROWTH SITKA SPRUCE DECOMPOSES IN A COASTAL FOREST ON CAPE FALCON.

FACING PAGE: FOXGLOVE BLOOM ON THE SLOPES OF CASCADE HEAD WHILE THE SALMON RIVER FLOWS INTO THE SEA BELOW.

THREE ARCH ROCKS

Sea stacks or offshore rocks—some big enough to be called islands—result from the surf's endless erosion of land. Here's how it happens: as the waves constantly batter the shore, they wash away the softer rocks and soil. Ultimately the ocean encroaches on the shoreline and leaves only the hardiest rocks as capes and headlands. Relentless, the waves finally chew away behind the rocky promontories and sometimes create tunneled arches that eventually cave in, leaving islands of resistant rock surrounded by sea.

Formed in this way, Three Arch Rocks is one of the premier seabird sanctuaries on the West Coast. Used for roosting and nesting, the rocks host up to 220,000 common murres and Brandt's cormorants, and 4,000 clown-faced tufted puffins.

These rocks were not always the monuments to life they are today. In the early 1900s a tour operator took boatloads of men around the islands each week for the sole purpose of joy-shooting, leaving hundreds of dead birds where they lay. Photographers William Finley and Herman Bohlman publicized the gristly scene and helped lead the effort that stopped the pointless slaughter. President Theodore Roosevelt designated Three Arch Rocks as part of a national wildlife refuge in 1907.

SITKA SPRUCE

The Sitka spruce is the king of the coast, found among thirty different species of conifers along Oregon's western limits and in the Siskiyou Mountains in the southwestern corner of the state. This evergreen needs large doses of magnesium—an element that just happens to be abundant in the mist of seawater. Growing to a diameter of eight feet and a height of 200 feet, the sharp-needled spruce thrives at ocean's edge from Oregon through Washington and across southern Alaska. There it reigns as the westernmost tree on our Pacific shore; beyond the final Sitka grove on Kodiak Island, no trees of any kind can be found.

Highly prized for its strong, lightweight wood, nearly all the original spruce in Oregon was cut, but small old groves remain at Cape Sebastian, Cascade Head, Cape Lookout, Meares Head, and a few other protected parks and reserves.

TIDEPOOLS INVITE EXPLORATION AT OCEANSIDE BEACH, WITH THREE ARCH ROCKS JUST OFFSHORE.

SITKA SPRUCE THRIVE IN THE MISTY ATMOSPHERE AT OSWALD WEST STATE PARK.

Sand and Rocks

The landscape of the coast owes to powerful seismic forces causing countless earthquakes over the millennia. Geologists now know that the earth is divided into plates—large sections of the crust that float on top of semi-liquid rock underneath. The North American Plate is slowly inching westward. But not far out into the Pacific, the Juan de Fuca Plate is a smaller section of crust hidden undersea and migrating eastward. Composed mostly of dense volcanic rock, it is heavier than the North American Plate, so where the two collide, it's pushed underneath. In the process, lighter rocks such as sandstones are scraped off the top of the incoming plate and slathered against the advancing western edge of North America. Millions of years of pile-up have created Oregon's coastal mountains.

The rocks that we see when strolling along the Pacific have come from the ancient undersea accumulations of sediment and lava. Through ongoing earthquakes, more will arrive. Oregon is still in the process of being made and remade all the time.

Bedrock outcrops on the central coast offer clues about the fascinating geologic forces that have shaped the western slope of Oregon.

THE STORMS OF WINTER BRING STONES, SAND, SCRAPS OF DRIFTWOOD, AND BROKEN SEA PALMS TO SHORE.

GRAVEL AND DRIFTWOOD

The tidal zone always has stories to tell, its mysteries never fully solved. Subject to great forces of transport and dispersal, simple bits of gravel, driftwood, and sealife have traveled unknown distances through days, decades, or millennia to finally arrive here at our beach. The gravel may have washed down an Oregon river and into the sea, where waves sorted it by size and shape and cast it back up onto the beach like a colorful set of marbles. The broken limb of sea palm—an aquatic algae that grows on rocks where the tides forcefully wash in and out—may have been uprooted nearby during the last windy storm. The rounded edges of driftwood attest to erosion against sand and rock during many miles and months spent in water. The journey of this wood began in the forest, when a branch or whole tree fell into a stream, which flushed it out to sea where the surf smoothed its edges with the same physics that more slowly contour rocks into discs and eggs. The wood and the stones both are carved smaller and smaller until ultimately nothing is left but a single fiber or a single grain of sand.

While the nature of the coast is as stable as bedrock and as timeless as the tides, it's also a medium for transient delicacies and diminutive wonders, here today, gone tomorrow.

THE YAQUINA HEAD LIGHTHOUSE RISES FROM HEADLANDS
ON THE CENTRAL COAST NEAR NEWPORT.

YAQUINA HEAD

Battered by winds so domineering that even the pioneering Sitka spruce won't grow, Yaquina Head catches the full brunt of Pacific storms. The ninety-three-foot lighthouse there is the tallest in Oregon. Since it first opened in 1873 it has signaled danger, warning "stay away" to sailors who navigated the hazardous coast.

After installing automated beacons in the 1960s, the Coast Guard began transferring Oregon's lighthouses to other agencies for maintenance as historic sites, and all nine have been enrolled in the National Register of Historic Places. Visitors enjoy public tours here at Yaquina Head and also at lighthouses at Cape Blanco, Heceta Head, and the mouth of the Umpqua River.

FISHING BOATS

The great, age-old profession of commercial fishing is still alive on the Oregon coast. Coos Bay, Newport, Astoria, and smaller ports harbor colorful fleets of trollers, crabbers, long-liners, and the destructive seabottom-scraping trawlers—big metal boats that most fishermen call draggers. Each uses a different technique and catches different kinds of fish—salmon, tuna, crab, shrimp, and groundfish.

Most of the boats in this picture are trollers, which ply the offshore waters while pulling eight or ten baited lines, much as a sport fisherman in a lake might do. Unlike trawling, long-lining, or seining, trolling allows the fish to be caught live without damaging its tissues. The fish can immediately be frozen for freshness. The much-savored albacore tuna and king salmon are taken this way. Intrepid fishermen routinely pilot their modest boats a hundred miles out in the sea and work for ten or twelve days before returning home or to other ports.

The ocean fishery, however, is only a ghost of what it once was, and the sustainability of many fish populations is in peril. Dams have blocked the routes of the salmon so that they cannot reach their spawning grounds. Over-fishing at sea has depleted many stocks of fish once considered so plentiful that nobody believed they could ever be exhausted. Erosion caused by logging, farming, and ranching has ruined many of the clear, gravel-bottomed streams needed for spawning. The coho salmon are a good example of the decline: in the 1970s coho caught in the Pacific Northwest generated $70 million a year in direct personal income, but today no coho can legally be caught in Oregon and California. Biologists believe that their future viability depends on the protection of habitat.

COMMERCIAL FISHERMEN MOOR THEIR BOATS AT COOS BAY,
ONE OF THE THREE LARGEST FISHING HARBORS IN THE STATE.

POWERFUL COASTAL WINDS SHAPE UNDULANT SAND DUNES; HAYSTACK ROCK, NEAR CANNON BEACH, RISES IN THE DISTANCE.

SAND DUNES

After the rivers wash sand down to the sea, and after the surf tosses it back up onto the beaches, the heady winds of the Oregon coast pile it up into dunes that can reach a whopping 165 feet in height. The Coos Bay complex, running northward for sixty miles to Heceta Head, is the largest coastal dune accumulation in the country. These great dunes can migrate landward fifteen feet per year until the winds are buffered and forests begin to grow. The sand effectively isolates inland areas from the sea, incidentally damming small creeks and trapping the water to create valuable wetlands.

PITCHER PLANTS

The pitcher plant—known to botanists as *Darlingtonia californica*—is one of the more fascinating wildflowers found in wetlands along the Pacific coast. Darlingtonia grows on serpentine—a blue-green mineral originating undersea and found in many of the rocks of the Coast Range. The soil weathering from this mineral tests high in magnesium, silica, and iron, while testing low in calcium, potassium, and the mandatory nitrogen—a difficult if not toxic combination for most plantlife, yet suitable for the unusual flora that have adapted.

The "carnivorous" pitcher plant gets the nutrients it needs from the bodies of insects. Sweet nectar lures the bugs into an opening on the underside of the plant's hood, then slippery interior walls studded with downward-pointing hairs prevent escape. The insect ends up drowning in a pool of water at the base of the stem. Microscopic organisms living in the water consume the insect and release essential nutrients that are absorbed by the plant.

PITCHER PLANTS AT THE DARLINGTONIA BOTANICAL GARDENS NORTH OF FLORENCE THRIVE IN WETLANDS, VALUABLE FOR THEIR DIVERSITY OF LIFE.

SUNSET BAY STATE PARK

Much of Oregon's coast is protected in sixty-six state-park sites. One of the finest collections of parks anywhere in America, these cover wild wooded headlands and also broad swaths of beach and dune.

Established mostly between 1929 and 1950, the coastal parks were largely the work of Samuel H. Boardman, who directed an acquisition effort that ultimately bought 51,000 acres in 495 transactions statewide. The crowning legacy of this man's far-sighted career is Boardman State Park, which protects ten miles of the most rugged seashore in southern Oregon.

In 1964 the state parks division renewed its commitment to the public by launching a program to establish access to beaches at roughly three-mile intervals. While most of America's coastline elsewhere has fallen into private ownership, two-thirds of Oregon's beaches are publicly owned.

One could easily spend an entire summer getting to know the varied state parks along the coast. For that matter, one could spend a lifetime. Shown in this picture, Sunset Bay State Park offers a three-mile headland trail and one of the safer swimming beaches, for hearty souls willing to brave the shockingly cold water.

A SHORE PINE GROWS AT THE EDGE OF A FOGGY WETLAND IN BULLARDS BEACH STATE PARK.

FOG AND BEDROCK

While rain is plentiful along the Oregon coast in winter, fog refreshingly dampens the coast in summer, especially in mornings before the sun burns it off.

The fog's prevalence owes to a weather system called the Pacific High, a high-pressure dome that consistently resides in the north Pacific during summer months. Blowing from the northwest, winds are strong enough to push water at the ocean's surface and create a southbound current, which sweeps cool water down from the north and also creates turbulence that draws very cold water from ocean depths in a process called upwelling. As a result, the surface water is markedly chilled, and when the warmer air of summertime comes in contact with it, the water abruptly cools the lowest layer of air to its dew point, which causes invisible water vapor to condense into fog. When the Pacific High of northwestern winds subsides, the upwelling decreases as well, and the fog is subdued, yielding sunny days that surely describe paradise on the Oregon coast.

DRIFTWOOD

Fantastic piles of logs end up along the seashore after trees die and fall into rivers, float out to sea on the roaring crests of floods, and then get tossed ashore again by winter storms. Not just big flotsam, these logs play a vital role in the life of Oregon's rivers and shores.

First, when they fall into the streams, they create shelter and habitat for fish, invertebrates, and insects fundamental to the greater food chain. They create temporary blockages that enhance pools and riffles, which are both crucial to the health of streams. Feeding on the wood, insects break it down into carbon-rich byproducts with minerals and nutrients required by other life in the streams, rivers, estuaries, and even deep waters of the sea. Plentiful salmon runs actually depend on large dead trees being in the streams.

Once washed out to sea, the logs might drift for days, months, or years, but eventually they are blown back toward shore. There the floating logs batter rocks and create disturbed areas that are important to tidal creatures waiting to colonize on hard, rocky surfaces periodically scraped clean by the logs. Eventually deposited high-and-dry by the combined forces of spring tide and storm surf, or perhaps even by a tidal wave or tsunami, the logs create habitat for wildlife on the beach—and good fodder for photographers as well.

SUNSET BAY NEAR CHARLESTON IS ONE OF MANY STATE PARKS PROTECTING THE OREGON COAST.

SANDSTONE WEATHERS IN THE RAIN AND SURF AT SHORE ACRES STATE PARK NEAR CHARLESTON.

DRIFTWOOD DECORATES THE BEACH AT CAPE BLANCO NEAR PORT ORFORD.

A CRESCENT MOON SETS TOWARD THE HORIZON AT HECETA HEAD.

SEA STACKS AT HECETA HEAD

These rocky remains of headlands are typical along the Oregon coast. If you take a short walk between April and August on the cliffs near the Heceta Head Lighthouse, you'll see that the rocks are covered with common murres and Brandt's cormorants, along with lesser numbers of brown pelicans and other seabirds. The sea stacks make ideal habitat because they are close to the food source of these fish-eating birds, yet they offer refuge from predators living on the mainland or in the water.

More than 1,700 islands dot the offshore waters and collectively form the Oregon Islands National Wildlife Refuge. These protected outliers offer nesting and roosting habitat for petrels, auklets, puffins, guillemots, oystercatchers, gulls, peregrine falcons, brown pelicans, bald eagles, and the rare Aleutian Canada goose. Both Steller and California sea lions as well as harbor seals haul out to rest and warm on the ground floor of the rocks.

A POPULAR STOP FOR COASTAL TRAVELERS, THE HECETA HEAD
LIGHTHOUSE BRIGHTENS THE TWILIGHT HOUR.

HECETA HEAD LIGHTHOUSE

The most photographed landmark on Oregon's coast, this lighthouse
north of Florence stands on the great promontory of Heceta Head.
The distinctive fifty-six-foot tower was first illuminated in 1894, and its
beacon can still be seen from twenty-one miles offshore, fog and
rainstorms permitting.

CAPE BLANCO LIGHTHOUSE

This photogenic lighthouse is the oldest lighthouse in Oregon. Built
in 1870 to aid shipping in the lumber and gold mining industries, it
rises atop the remarkable Cape Blanco, which juts out farther west
than any other point on the Oregon coast. South of Canada, only the
northern thirty-five miles of Washington extend farther.

Seismically superlative as well, the cape marks the triple junction where the North American, Gorda, and Juan de Fuca Plates all
converge in a bumpercar of earthquake activity. Extremely large
tremors occur near the Oregon coast every 300 years or so. The last
one happened in about 1700.

Cape Blanco also has the windiest weather in Oregon and some
of the windiest weather ever recorded on the coasts of America.
Seventy miles per hour is not uncommon, with stronger gusts too
powerful to stand up in.

Braving the Cape's stiff breeze on a misty summer night, I once
walked south from Blanco on a spacious sandy beach to the mouth of
the Elk River, which slices through a sandbar and into the Pacific. A
bald eagle cried overhead. An osprey dove and caught three-inch-long
fish in its talons. As I returned at dusk, the lighthouse flashed in cycle,
its beam illumined in fog and looking like a comet in the sky.

THE CAPE BLANCO LIGHTHOUSE, BUILT IN 1870, MARKS THE
WESTERNMOST POINT IN OREGON.

ELK RIVER

One of the truly splendid rivers of the West Coast, the Elk tumbles from the Coast Range through gorges, over churning rapids, and beneath the shade of ancient forests. Though depleted from their original numbers, the salmon here still rate among the healthiest runs on the Pacific Coast, south of Canada.

Much of this basin has been heavily logged, but 17,200 acres are now protected as the Grassy Knob Wilderness—part of a lonely 4 percent of the Oregon Coast Range forest that remains uncut. All the more valuable for its scarcity, these forests offer shelter to the endangered spotted owl and to the marbled murrelet—a bird that feeds at sea but nests in old timber as far as thirty miles inland. Scores of other species also depend on the old-growth forests. Tall stands of Douglas fir and the increasingly rare Port Orford cedar blanket steep slopes north of the river and nourish tributaries that provide spawning habitat for the salmon and steelhead swimming up from the sea.

RHODODENDRONS, FIRS, AND REDWOODS

The showy blossoms of the Pacific rhododendron bloom pink and red in the spring and make a colorful garden in the mixed coniferous forest of western hemlock, Port Orford cedar, Douglas fir, and redwood.

The remarkable redwoods extend from the Big Sur coast of California to southern Oregon. The tallest trees in the world, they top out at 365 feet. An arboreal embodiment of the West Coast, they need both winter rains and summer fog to survive, and so their range overlaps that of the Pacific High's oceanic upwelling and related fog. Reaching far into the sky, the redwood branches harvest the fog by accumulating droplets on their needles and then dripping these droplets onto the ground, effectively watering the tree through the dry months of summer. Up to thirty inches of water a year is collected this way. Lacking efficient root hairs, the redwoods cannot

RHODODENDRONS BLOOM IN THIS DOUGLAS FIR AND REDWOOD FOREST NEAR LOEB STATE PARK ALONG THE CHETCO RIVER.

tap soil moisture as well as other conifers do, and so they depend heavily on fog for a nearly continuous water supply.

The northernmost groves of redwoods cluster along a few streams of the southern Oregon Coast Range. Here near the Chetco River in the Siskiyou National Forest, towering redwoods live up to 800 years.

THE ELK RIVER, JEWEL OF THE OREGON COAST RANGE, FLOWS PAST THE GRASSY KNOB WILDERNESS,
SPARED FROM LOGGING BY THE FORESIGHT OF LOCAL CONSERVATIONISTS.

MINIATURE LUPINE BLANKETS THE GROUND WITH
TABLE ROCK IN THE BACKGROUND.

TABLE ROCK

On the eastern side of the coastal mountains, rising as a high bluff
above the Rogue River Valley, Table Rock is what remains of an
ancient volcanic flow that spread through southern Oregon nearly
10 million years ago, filling the low-lying river valley. Older and softer
rock surrounding the hardened lava eventually eroded, ironically
leaving the lava-filled riverbed as the new high ground, 800 feet above
the current floor of the Rogue River Valley.

    Cutting its way from the upper Cascade Mountains to Gold
Beach, the Rogue is one of few rivers that crosscut the entire way
through the Coast Range. In the background of this photo, the
Siskiyou Mountains rumple southward. Attached in the geologic past
to both the Sierra Nevada of California and Blue Mountains of
central Oregon, this range hosts more conifer species than any other
region in the world.

ANDESITE CLIFFS OF LOWER TABLE ROCK RISE UP FROM THE
ROGUE VALLEY NEAR MEDFORD.

ABOVE: WHITE POPCORN FLOWER BLOOMS AT THE AGATE DESERT PRESERVE NORTH OF MEDFORD.

FACING PAGE: SILVERLEAF MANZANITA GROWS IN DENSE THICKETS.

FLORA OF TABLE ROCK

Enduring intensely hot summers in this interior basin—east of the Coast Range but west of the high Cascades—Table Rock hosts a shrubby, drought-resistant community of plants called chaparral, including madrone, ceanothus, and manzanita. With probing tap-roots to glean deep-soil moisture during the summer and also with surface roots to absorb rainfall whenever it occurs, the brushy chaparral is well adapted to both heat and dryness. Quickly building up tinderbox-litter in leaves, limbs, and trunks, the chaparral has evolved by burning frequently. In fact, it depends on periodic lightening-caused fires; burning releases nutrients locked in the dead material and returns them to the soil, where they can nurture new growth.

Andesite and Annual Grasses

This harsh, lava-based landscape at the eastern border of the coastal mountains typifies the enormous volcanic influences that have shaped the rest of Oregon. Most of the land of this state was formed during eruptions from deep in the earth and was shaped by the great forces of ice and water that followed.

The Siskiyou Mountains, rich with biological diversity, rise across the skyline to the south of Table Rock.

CHAPTER 2

THE GREATEST GORGE

Pathway to the Interior

Known as the Great River of the West, the Columbia is the largest waterway draining into the Pacific Ocean from the Americas. Recently I spent an entire summer exploring the Columbia, and after seeing the far-flung pieces and learning how they fit together, the view of the mature river here at the Columbia Gorge will always look different to me. It's not just big and beautiful but also intricate, complex, and compromised.

From its source in British Columbia, the river first flows down past the Canadian Rockies. Many people aren't even aware that the Columbia begins in Canada, though in fact 40 percent of its total mileage lies there. Crossing the international border, the river enters a chain of reservoirs that stair-step down to tidewater, back-to-back and continuous except for one surviving free-flowing reach of fifty miles. The water passes through sagebrush-steppe drylands and bunchgrass prairies as it defines the boundary between Washington and Oregon. And then, with a massive flow including hundreds of tributaries from dozens of mountain ranges, the great river approaches the upper entrance to the Gorge.

A scenic highlight to the waterway's 1,240-mile-long journey, the Columbia Gorge extends for eighty-three miles from The Dalles—on the eastern side of the Cascade Mountains—to Troutdale, near Portland.

Like everything worthwhile, the formation of the Gorge took time. As the volcanoes of the Cascades arose, the river constantly and patiently crosscut its way through successive barriers of rock, maintaining its Pacific-bound path.

Sometimes the river is not so patient. Upstream in today's Montana, a backwater the size of Lake Michigan was formed by a dam of ice during the Pleistocene, and when it gave way, an unimaginable torrent of water carrying more flow than all the rivers on earth washed across the desert of eastern Washington to the head of the Gorge. Then the 800-foot wall of water tore out the remarkable trench we see today. Just downstream, the surge of flood-flow buried the site of Portland 400 feet deep. Different versions of this cataclysm happened thirty-five times as the ice dams re-formed and re-broke.

The carving has stopped for now because the Columbia is impounded by Bonneville Dam near tidewater. This dam and others have buried the rapids and impeded the salmon in their efforts to reach spawning grounds in headwater streams and return to the ocean as young smolts. The river no longer flows freely, but some of the grandeur of the Gorge remains, with its steep rise of forested slopes and the rush of tributary streams bubbling down from highcountry.

LUPINE AND ARROWLEAF BALSAMROOT BLOOM ABOVE THE COLUMBIA RIVER.

LATOURELL FALLS DROPS OVER BASALT CLIFFS AT GUY W. TALBOT STATE PARK ON THE WEST END OF THE COLUMBIA RIVER GORGE.

LOWER MULTNOMAH FALLS

Remote cascades, basalt cliffs, draperies of lichen, and cushions of moss decorate the Columbia River Gorge. More waterfalls splash down from mountainsides in the Gorge than in any other place in America. Because the ponderous flows and cataclysmic floods of the great river carved through the region's lava so quickly and effectively, the smaller streams were left hanging high, and to meet the river they must now plunge over vertical faces of dark volcanic basalt.

There's something universally delightful about standing so close to a waterfall that the sound drowns out all conversation and the mist washes your face and fills your lungs with welcome moisture. Beyond these joys, I've wondered why waterfalls are so appealing. Of course they are beautiful, and they move with animation that really captures the eye. But perhaps it's the way water is so utterly transformed that's most captivating for me. For one brief instant the water leaves itself and becomes part of the air, flying through space.

The most visited site in the Gorge, Multnomah Falls drops in two pitches. A total descent of 620 feet makes it the fourth-highest waterfall in America. Trails to the base and to the top introduce hikers to this unrepeatable place and to the wonders of a stream of water that has—for a few spectacular seconds—taken flight.

ONE OF THE MOST VISITED NATURAL SITES IN OREGON, MULTNOMAH FALLS PLUNGES DOWN FROM ITS HEADWATERS ON LARCH MOUNTAIN.

JAPANESE GARDEN

One of the finer re-creations of a classical Japanese formal garden, this site in Portland's Washington Park is maintained with care and invites visitors of all cultures to quietly enjoy and contemplate the simple beauties of nature—wild or tame.

The Japanese garden in Washington Park is just one special place in Portland's 7,000-acre park system. In this cultured city where the Willamette River meets the Columbia, Forest Park stretches for seven miles, the largest urban woodland park in America. The Crystal Springs Garden sports 2,500 flowering rhododendrons in springtime. Mount Tabor Park rises as a high landmark on the eastern side of the city—one of seventy-eight expired volcanoes in the greater urban area. Walking up its forested slopes on winding trails is a daily practice of Portlanders who live nearby.

A JAPANESE GARDEN IN WASHINGTON PARK, PORTLAND, INVITES URBAN VISITORS TO STROLL AND RELAX.

EAGLE CREEK OFFERS ONE OF THE FINER HIKES IN THE COLUMBIA GORGE, WITH TRAILS THAT CONNECT
TO MOUNT HOOD AND TO OTHER HEIGHTS OF THE CASCADE MOUNTAINS.

EAGLE CREEK

Foaming over seven waterfalls and rushing through deep woodlands of the Mount Hood National Forest, Eagle Creek is just one sample of the magnificent system of national forest land in Oregon. Covering one-fourth of the state, thirteen national forests were reserved from development early in the 1900s and now form an invaluable network of public land. Open for hiking, hunting, fishing, and a host of other outdoor recreation activities, this coveted estate of public land is the birthright of every Oregonian.

While most of the national forest system has been logged at least once, old-growth forests remain in parts of the Eagle Creek watershed, and big trees still shade the stream. The headwaters, clad in noble fir and western hemlock, lie in the Columbia Wilderness Area. Statewide only 2 million of Oregon's 60 million acres are safeguarded as wilderness—a federal designation that prevents further logging, road building, and motor-vehicle use. Another 4 million acres of publicly owned land have wilderness qualities but are not yet protected.

PUNCHBOWL FALLS

While unique sites such as Punchbowl Falls are part of Mount Hood National Forest, much of the land within the Columbia Gorge was turned over to private ownership in the 1800s and has been logged, mined for rock and gravel, or developed with houses and commercial businesses. Major highways and railroads have crowded both the north and south shores. Even so, a place of singular beauty remained, leading citizens to struggle for years to establish the Columbia Gorge National Scenic Area. With painterly views and the historical legacies of both Lewis and Clark and the Oregon Trail, the Gorge is home to sixty kinds of wildlife listed as endangered, threatened, or imperiled. From a biological standpoint alone, it's one of the most important landscapes in Oregon.

The National Scenic Area designation in 1986 led to the creation of a commission appointed by local governments and the states of Oregon and Washington and to the adoption of a plan for preserving the good looks of the place. New development is encouraged in urban areas, some development is allowed in buffer zones, and only less obtrusive development is permitted on 35 percent of the land having the greatest scenic importance. Yet since 1986, 600 houses have been built in places that were supposed to have been protected. Some of the local governments oppose the National Scenic Area regulations and constantly seek loopholes in the plan intended to safeguard the best of what the Gorge has to offer.

PUNCHBOWL FALLS TYPIFIES THE SCENIC WONDERS OF THE COLUMBIA RIVER GORGE.

CHERRY TREES DOT THE HILLS NEAR MOSIER IN THE DRIER, EASTERN REACHES OF THE GORGE.

PEAR AND CHERRY ORCHARDS

It's the fascinating interplay of climate and landscape that makes the Gorge such a bountiful fruit-growing region. The prevailing winds from the west bring abundant rainfall to the Oregon coast and to the Cascade Mountains, but as those winds push their cloud masses over the Cascade crest, the bulk of the moisture falls out, leaving little for the drier, eastern side. Accentuating the climatic difference, the winds that descend the east slope of the Cascades warm up, and when they do, they're able to cling to whatever moisture remains. As a result, the eighty-three-mile journey through the Columbia River Gorge presents one of the more abrupt transitions in climate found anywhere. The west side receives seventy-five inches of precipitation—almost a rainforest—while the east side gets twelve inches—almost a desert.

Orchards blossom here halfway through the Gorge. Similarly past the mid-point, Oregon white oak replaces the rain-loving bigleaf maple. Sun-loving ponderosa pine replaces moisture-tuned red cedar. For a lift of mood and a change of pace during the rainy days of winter, which linger month after month after month, Portlanders drive a couple of hours and emerge in the sunny climes of eastern Oregon.

Pear trees bloom with Mount Hood in the background.

ARROWLEAF BALSAMROOT

One of the showiest flowers in the West, arrowleaf balsamroot, pictured here at the Tom McCall Nature Preserve, blankets rich volcanic soils in drier reaches of the Gorge. Today we take delight in these dazzling fields, but for the Indians, the blooms were much more than a floral display. The balsamroot's leaves were eaten raw, young flower stems peeled and snacked upon, and roots steamed to soften their toughness. After roasting, the sunflower-like seeds were pounded into flour. Deer and elk relish the tender shoots, and deer and elk were another important part of the original Oregonians' diet.

The balsamroot is just one of 800 species of native plants found in the Gorge; the importance of its varied life matches the beauty of its waterfalls and the grandeur of its cliffs.

This 230-acre Nature Conservancy preserve with hawks and eagles soaring overhead is named for Oregon's incomparable Tom McCall, governor from 1967 to 1974. One of the most colorful figures in the political world of his day, McCall was also one of the most effective governors of all time in passing legislation to protect the environment, including exemplary efforts to curb urban sprawl, to preserve countrysides and farmland, and to keep development from cluttering the seashore. With his reforms under siege ever since he left office, Oregonians continuously battle to save Tom McCall's legacy.

OREGON WHITE OAK

A stately hardwood tree found in eastern reaches of the Gorge and in the Willamette Valley, as well as in the upper Umpqua and Rogue basins to the south, the Oregon white oak branches out over grasslands and wildflower hillsides. I love to sit on the ground and lean against the solid backrest of a giant oak, its girthy arms reaching up for the sky, its leaves a fluttering ceiling overhead. But beyond offering these kinds of pleasures, oak woodlands and their grassy savannas are vital for dozens of breeding bird species and 200 kinds of wildlife.

As fundamental as they are to the natural makeup of Oregon, oak woodlands are one of the most threatened habitats in the state. Because of farming, urban development, and the suppression of natural fires that once burned frequently but beneficially in the oaks' dry niche, these keystone trees have disappeared from 95 percent of their native range, and the birds and wildlife that depend on them are disappearing as well. The Nature Conservancy and other groups have launched programs aimed at saving the best of the oak savanna and restoring what they can.

ABOVE: ARROWLEAF BALSAMROOT AND LUPINE BURST INTO BLOOM AT THE TOM MCCALL NATURE PRESERVE.

FACING PAGE: OREGON WHITE OAKS HAVE BEEN ELIMINATED FROM MUCH OF THEIR RANGE BUT THRIVE HERE IN THE EASTERN REACHES OF THE GORGE.

WAHKEENA CREEK

Tumbling toward the Columbia in autumn, Wahkeena Creek rushes over mossy rocks covered by yellow leaves of the bigleaf maple. One of the hardwood mainstays in a mostly-coniferous forest, this maple grows into broad umbrellas of canopy spreading from girthy trunks two and three feet in diameter. The limbs of this maple hold more mosses, lichens, and other epiphytic plants than any other species of tree in the Northwest; the weight of piggybacking vegetation can equal four times that of the maple's own leaves. Mosses high in the trees grow so thick that they produce soil nursing an aerial garden of licorice ferns.

SWORD FERNS

Because they reproduce by spores rather than better-protected seeds, ferns need to grow on moist ground, and there's plenty of that in the Columbia Gorge. One of the more common among forty fern species that green the Northwest, these sword ferns grace the forest with their bouquet of fronds at Horsetail Falls.

A backyard escape for urbanites on the west side of the mountains—a destination for travelers from all over the nation—the Columbia River Gorge offers the allure of a world apart and a wildness lying close to the homes and the hearts of many Oregonians.

ABOVE: AUTUMN LEAVES FALL AT THE EDGE OF WAHKEENA CREEK IN THE COLUMBIA GORGE.

FACING PAGE: SWORD FERNS COLLECT BIGLEAF MAPLE LEAVES AT THE BASE OF HORSETAIL FALLS WEST OF AINSWORTH STATE PARK.

OVERLEAF: THE COLUMBIA, LARGEST RIVER IN THE AMERICAN WEST, CARVED ITS SIGNATURE GORGE HERE AT THE NORTHERN BORDER OF OREGON.

CHAPTER 3

THE CASCADE RANGE

Brilliant Peaks and Ancient Forests

Running the length of the state, from the banks of the Columbia to the California border and beyond, the Cascade Mountains rise as the ultimate crown of Oregon. They are the source of so much. Their high peaks and ridges force the soggy clouds of the Pacific up and up, which cools them and produces rain and snow. Prodigious runoff into rivers and aquifers provides water upon which everyone depends. Even the soil of our farms and backyards is delivered in part by the Cascade rivers, wearing away at the highcountry and the foothills, and washing fertile dirt down to settle in the Willamette and connected valleys—the breadbasket of the Northwest.

Among the highest peaks we find the cone-shaped or broken-tooth tops of Hood, Jefferson, Three Fingered Jack, Washington, North Sister, Middle Sister, South Sister, Bachelor, Thielson, and McLoughlin. Each is a result of volcanism deep within the earth—a phenomenon beginning with the collision of the North American Plate and offshore terranes—the same geologic genesis that formed the seashore and Coast Range of chapter 1. But here, the story takes a new and dramatic twist.

As we saw at the coast, the oceanic terranes are driven under the more buoyant North American Plate. And once subducted, they don't stop. They continue moving with a trajectory that angles them both downward toward the inner earth and also eastward as a wedge beneath the encroaching continent. After traveling a hundred miles in that direction, they've reached enough depth in the semi-liquid interior of the earth that the oceanic rocks turn to molten lava. This expands as it becomes hotter and ultimately jettisons upward and erupts through vents in the surface of the earth. Lava, pumice, and ash spread across the land and build up the quintessential cones of volcanoes. Today these young mountains glean moisture from the passing Pacific storms and tower over the rest of Oregon with glorious white coats of snow.

At 9,065 feet above sea level, Mount Bachelor is one of the most visited Cascade peaks because a ski area has been built there. Unlike slopes at lower elevations where the snow comes down wet and slushy, Bachelor sees 300 inches of mostly cold, dry snow—just right for powder skiing.

ONE OF THE GREAT STRATO-VOLCANOES OF THE CASCADES, MOUNT BACHELOR TOWERS OVER TODD LAKE IN CENTRAL OREGON.

MOUNT HOOD

Highest among the Oregon Cascades, Mount Hood rises to 11,235 feet. I will never forget my first view of this monumental yet elegant mountain. A teenage hitchhiker at the time, I had arrived in the middle of the night in the desert near the Deschutes River and unrolled my sleeping bag in the sagebrush. When I awoke in the morning, the first golden light of the day shone on the pudding of snowfields and crushed ice of fractured glacial slopes—so high, so beautiful, so perfect. Having had no idea that the mountain was there at all, I could only stare in amazement at Hood's unexpected but powerful charisma.

Later that summer I caught a ride one weekend to Timberline Lodge, stepped out of the car at snowline, and began walking. My only goal was to see all that I could of this captivating peak. After several hours I came to a steep rise followed by a crevasse. The summit still loomed far above, starkly white, its greatness overwhelming and arresting. I turned and started back down.

Mount Hood might well be the most memorable landmark of the entire state as it rises celestially from the horizon in Portland. It can be seen from countless other lookouts, both east and west of the Cascade crest. With eleven glaciers packed in against steep rocky faces, with national forest surrounding this radial gem, and with rivers including the Sandy, Salmon, White, and Hood streaming off dazzling flowered slopes, Mount Hood draws Oregonians and visitors alike to its lofty beauty.

FACING PAGE: FRESH WINTER SNOWS CATCH SUNSET LIGHT ON MOUNT HOOD.

LEFT: TIMBERLINE LODGE OFFERS WARM SHELTER AT THE BASE OF MOUNT HOOD.

TIMBERLINE LODGE

Built by the New Deal's Works Progress Administration (WPA) in 1937, Timberline Lodge still hosts visitors to the slippery snowfields of Mount Hood. Of classic rustic design, this National Historic Landmark features hand-crafted timbers and furnishings. Artisans laid off during the Great Depression went to work for the WPA carving owls and bears for fixtures, and even weaving rugs in custom designs.

In the 1920s, in one of the earliest efforts to protect a mountaintop in America, a Portland based climbing club called the Mazamas fought off a proposal to build a tram to the top of the mountain. Ski lifts were later built to lower points, and now those slopes are open longer than any other downhill ski area in the country. The lifts close for only two weeks in October. Each year 10,000 climbers try to reach the summit—the second-most climbed snowpeak in the world.

ABOVE: CLARKIA BLOOMS IN THE VALLEY OF THE LITTLE RIVER.

FACING PAGE: BIGLEAF MAPLES FRAME SOUTH FALLS IN SILVER FALLS STATE PARK, ON THE WEST SLOPE OF THE CASCADES.

SILVER FALLS

Silver Falls plunges 177 feet on its way to the Willamette Valley. Nine other falls highlight this watercourse.

Hundreds of other streams like Silver Creek feed ten major rivers draining the Oregon Cascades. The Sandy, Clackamas, Santiam, McKenzie, Umpqua, and Rogue flow down west slopes from snowy peaks and through the wide belt of evergreens. On the drier east side, much of the snowmelt seeps into porous volcanic conduits and then reemerges as springflows that feed the Hood, Metolius, Deschutes, and Klamath Rivers. Together these streams form one of the premier river estates in America.

MOUNT WASHINGTON

The 7,794-foot summit of Mount Washington that we see today is only the core of a much larger shield volcano that once mounded up at this site. All but the most hardened lava has eroded away and washed downstream to become the soil of valleys below.

Washington's craggy asymmetrical summit is a plug of dense rock that usually indicates a volcano is extinct. The surrounding lava fields here are called the Black Wilderness because of their dark, rocky starkness. One hundred and twenty-five craters lie scattered as if a storm of sci-fi meteors had rained down on the mountains.

THE MOUNT JEFFERSON WILDERNESS

At 10,497 feet, Mount Jefferson is the second-highest peak in Oregon and the most difficult summit to climb, owing to the 400-foot pitch of rotten rock veering up to its lightening-rod top.

Wildflower gardens are typical of views from the Pacific Crest Trail as it passes near Mount Jefferson. A 2,638-mile route from Mexico to Canada, the famous footpath follows the Cascade chain for 424 miles in Oregon, skirting the highcountry.

Three Fingered Jack is also a highlight of the Mount Jefferson Wilderness. The cragginess of this 7,841-foot summit resulted from the inevitable forces of erosion. Outer layers of the peak have been stripped away by water, ice, and wind, leaving nothing at the summit but the hardened lava plug of an extinct volcano. Resistant ridges of rock flanking the top mark the location of dikes where lava was squeezed up between cracks in softer rock that has since crumbled away. The wilderness surrounding this Cascade landmark and the adjacent Mount Jefferson includes 150 lakes and artful splays of flowered meadows linking snowfields to deeply timbered slopes.

BIG LAKE REFLECTS THE LAVA SUMMIT OF
MOUNT WASHINGTON.

INDIAN PAINTBRUSH COLOR THE FOREGROUND IN THE MOUNT JEFFERSON WILDERNESS.

THREE FINGERED JACK RISES INTO SWIRLING CLOUDS.

LUPINE AND PAINTBRUSH

The blue flowers of lupine not only brighten meadow scenes throughout the Cascades, but they also enrich the soil. As a member of the legume family, which includes peas, snapdragons, and vetches, the lupine serves a valuable function in the ecology of its home.

Nitrogen is essential to all plants, and while the atmosphere is loaded with this element, the soil is not. As a result, much of life relies on certain species of plants to convert the nitrogen in the air into a form usable by other vegetation, and ultimately to animals that eat the plants. Microbes associated with the roots of legumes such as lupine convert the atmospheric nitrogen into forms that are then taken up by the plants and returned to the soil in a form that's ideal for other vegetation. Alder trees fix nitrogen as well, and without their pioneering work in building soil, the tall timberland of the Northwest might be just a land of scrub.

OPAL CREEK

The crystal-clear waters of Opal Creek flow through one of the finest old-growth forests in the Cascade Mountains of Oregon. Here the state's largest unlogged ancient-forest-watershed remains the way it has been through the ages, and one can stand among the tall giants and get a rare feel for what immortality must mean.

When I sit or lie beneath the giant trees, I try to imagine the centuries required to make that place what it is. With spongy soil buoying me up on the forest floor, I try to picture the generations that have succeeded each other, each building new life on the back of life that came before it, trees on top of trees, organic humus on top of older soil, clear down to the bedrock of lava that cooled when the age of volcanic eruptions came to an end.

With thousand-year-old trees reaching 250 feet into the sky and the mix of greenery along with presiding dead snags and fallen logs inundated in moss, I can understand how the harmonized pattern of life in nature goes on even when individual lives are lost. Centuries-old Douglas fir, western red cedar, and western hemlock shade the slopes and ravines in shadowy depths while shafts of light beam through the branches. In these remote groves the spotted owl, forest-cruising goshawk, and a host of other wildlife still thrive. Even a short stroll through these woods shows what vast reaches of the Cascade forest were once like.

Because most of the remaining tracts of old-growth are small, and fragmented by roads and development, the grove at Opal Creek became a battleground for conservationists who wanted to save the best that was left. They argued against a maze of roads and eighteen clear-cuts that were planned in the 1980s. The feisty array of volunteers and forest biologists organized as the Friends of Opal Creek, and in 1996 won congressional protection for 22,000 acres.

ABOVE: LUPINE AND PAINTBRUSH BRIGHTEN CANYON CREEK MEADOWS IN THE MOUNT JEFFERSON WILDERNESS.

FACING PAGE: THE ENCHANTING WATERS OF OPAL CREEK LIE AT THE HEART OF A GREAT ANCIENT FOREST PROTECTED BY CITIZEN ACTIVISTS IN THE 1990S.

Waldo Lake

High in the Cascades at 5,400 feet, Waldo Lake marks a key source of the Willamette River—the lifeline of Oregon. Waldo is the state's second-largest natural body of water, and its nearby wildlands hide the elusive and threatened wolverine, the fur-bearing fisher, the silently stalking mountain lion, a bugling herd of Roosevelt elk, and a whole foraging cast of black bears. The water here is famous for clarity because of the undisturbed wilderness that surrounds it. Trails of the area wind through ancient forests, including large groves of mountain hemlock.

After Waldo empties into the North Fork of the Middle Fork of the Willamette, tributaries converge to form the powerful main stem of the river, which feeds the agricultural heartland of Oregon and urban areas housing 70 percent of the state's population. Once a many-braided corridor replete with wetlands, sloughs, and whole arboretums of floodplain forests, the main-stem Willamette has been channelized and its banks armored with levees in order to expand farmland. Among many side effects of this heavy-handed reconstruction, the river now floods far worse than it did under the old regime, when its wetlands and multiple channels—in some places six miles wide—had the ability to absorb flood waters and then release them slowly. Instead, the river now flushes quickly with high runoff that overtops its banks and threatens towns and cities in its path. The Western Rivers Conservancy, based in Portland, seeks to buy and restore riverfront acreage so the river can accommodate its flood flows without causing so much damage. This group and others along the Willamette seek to reestablish some of the continuity of life in this great river, from Lake Waldo to the Columbia.

The summer sun sets at Waldo Lake.

VOLCANISM OF THE CASCADES IS EVERYWHERE EVIDENT AT THE McKENZIE PASS LAVA FLOW.

LAVA FLOW

Beneath the pyramidal peaks of the North and Middle Sister, the lava flow at McKenzie Pass may be the most recent lava flow in the continental United States. From Sims Butte, nine miles to the east, basalt and andesite oozed down after the last ice age, just a blink ago in geologic time, which explains why the lava looks like it might have arrived only yesterday.

Basalt comes from dark rocks of the interior earth, and when molten, it's like molasses—thick but fluid. As it moves across the ground, the surface of the lumbering flow cools and becomes chunky. Still pushed by the source of lava, the cooling and slowly solidifying surface cracks and jumbles like the breakup of ice in a river, and it mixes with the underlying flow to produce a razor-edged roughness. As long as the moving lava is about fifty feet thick, it keeps pushing the hardening rock at its surface, but when it becomes thinner than that, the flow begins to stop, eventually freezing in place.

Radiocarbon dating of ash left after trees were burned by the lava reveals that some of this deposit occurred 1,600 years ago. Other flows in the same area left no ash and so cannot be accurately dated, but they may have happened as recently as 400 years ago.

FOREST AND WINTER FOG

The mystery of winter is evident everywhere once you leave the highway and begin to explore on foot, on snowshoes, or on skis the depths of snowy woods in the Cascades. The storms arrive in waves from November through April and can drop their loads by the inch, by the foot, or by the yard. Santiam Pass, plowed all winter long, annually receives 250 to 700 inches of snow. Higher peaks get even more.

The storms might come in peaceful silence or in eye-squinting blizzards, but either way the snows of a long, demanding winter pile high. Travel in snowstorms or winter fog can be strangely disorienting; the sky takes on a dull blankness without direct sunlight to show direction. Tracks can be covered as fast as they are laid, yet the footprints of the coyote, pine marten, Douglas squirrel, and snowshoe hare might still be seen in all but the most severe hours of accumulation.

The whole world bleaches white, with somber greens of conifers fading into layers of gray. These trees have varying strategies for coping with the burdensome weight of snow. The hemlocks bend with the load until it sloughs off and the limbs spring back upright, undamaged. Incense cedar responds with a show of strength, the stiffness of its limbs supporting the heavy, wet weight. Subalpine fir grow as thin obelisks, pointed and narrow, so that the snow shrouds them in a protective blanket, and additional accumulations slide off.

Winter is the slow time of year when birds have fled to the south and the deer to lower terrain, when travelers tend to avoid driving over the passes because becoming stranded there is a real threat. Yet, at high elevations winter is the longest season, shaping much of life. To really know the mountains means knowing them through short days and long nights in the deep depths of snow.

NORTH FORK OF THE UMPQUA RIVER

Beginning in the mountain enclave of Diamond Lake, the North Fork of the Umpqua River drops 106 miles to the river's main stem below Roseburg. Not far below headwaters stair-stepped in cascades such as Toketee Falls, the North Fork is renowned as a steelhead stream. It poses the ultimate challenge to anglers because its sea-going rainbow trout are large and fight well, and because wading is difficult given the deep holes and steep banks. Also a favorite kayaking and canoeing river, the Umpqua draws whitewater boaters all summer long. The upper river offers twenty-six miles of superb trails leading to several old-growth forests that have been spared along the water's edge.

At the source of a river, where the flow just begins to gather in mountain rivulets or among rocks and bogs, I like to think about where the water will go. I like to imagine the adventure of flowing with the water, of traveling along with it the whole way to the sea.

Like hundreds of tributaries to the ten great rivers of the Cascades, the North Fork of the Umpqua begins here among chunky slabs of basalt. Farther downstream, among whitewater rapids and deep green pools, thirty-four miles of the North Umpqua have been designated in the National Wild and Scenic Rivers System. This congressional protection means that no dams can be built on the river and that additional logging in national forests must not damage the stream.

Far below these rocky beginnings, the Umpqua becomes the fifth-largest river in the state (only the Columbia, Snake, Willamette, and Santiam are larger). Offering one of the longer canoe routes possible on the West Coast, the main stem runs dam-free for 115 miles to the Pacific Ocean at Reedsport. There waters from far-flung reaches finally emerge in an estuary where seals swim up from the sea.

WINTER FOG DARKENS SANTIAM PASS.

Toketee Falls takes a ninety-foot drop over columnar basalt.

The North Fork of the Umpqua River begins in a landscape made of lava.

SUNSET LIGHT CREATES A SILHOUETTE OUT OF WIZARD ISLAND IN CRATER LAKE.

CRATER LAKE

A geologic wonder of the world, Crater Lake was formed in one of the more instantaneous rearrangements of rock and dirt ever known. At this site, Mount Mazama—comparable to Mount Hood—erupted in an explosion fifty times as powerful as Mount Saint Helens's pyroclastic blast in 1980. The land below Mount Mazama was layered in smothering depths of pumice. Wind-blown ash aggraded as a significant layer of soil in places as distant as Saskatchewan. Indians likely witnessed the fiery, smoky, dusty event, which occurred less than eight millennia ago. Much of what remained of the high peak collapsed into the cavity vacated by the explosion, the result being a caldera several thousand feet deep. This eventually collected 1,932 feet of snowmelt and became the deepest and bluest lake in the United States. Subsequent eruptions produced a crater within the caldera;

Wizard Island rises above lake level, topped by its own crater that once smoked with lava, fumes, and ash.

The eruption of Mount Mazama raises an interesting question: which Cascade peak is most likely to erupt next? Many of the volcanoes are still active, and the recent blast of Mount Saint Helens in southern Washington vividly illustrated nature's ability to rearrange entire mountains in truly astonishing ways.

McKenzie and Santiam Passes are considered among the most likely areas in the West to unleash new flows of lava. And Mazama itself may or may not be completely dead; other collapsed calderas, including Mount Shasta and the infamous Vesuvius, continued to erupt and rebuild themselves into mountains once again.

Snowdrifts harden to the wind at the rim of Crater Lake.

AT 8,929 FEET, MOUNT SCOTT RANKS AS THE HIGHEST POINT IN CRATER LAKE NATIONAL PARK.

EARLY VISITORS TO CRATER LAKE NAMED THIS ISLAND THE PHANTOM SHIP, SEEN HERE FROM KERR NOTCH ON THE EAST RIM.

MOUNT SCOTT AND THE PHANTOM SHIP

Crater Lake is Oregon's only national park, designated in 1902. Half a million visitors now come during a brief summer season. The road around the lake is snowed shut from October to June, though the road up to the rim is plowed all winter and invites cross-country skiers to cruise a wonderland of snowy slopes.

Surely everyone who has approached this spellbinding lake remembers the delightful shock of stepping up to the rim and looking down at the bluest color imaginable. I first did this when heavy snow still covered the ground and buried the mountain slopes around the lake. I had come to work at a summer job for the National Park Service and stood there scarcely believing what I saw. The lake was so

round, the slopes so steep, the water so *blue*. Later I checked in at headquarters and went to work as a carpenter's helper, garbage truck driver, and firefighter—a busy schedule full of jobs I enjoyed. But after work, the lake was always there, waiting for me, calling to me. On evenings I hiked up to high points around the caldera or to seldom visited recesses of the park, and on weekends I explored the streams that linked the park with the forests and mountains all around it. High in the Cascades, Crater Lake whetted my appetite for the rest of Oregon and stirred my interest in how its landforms and lifelines are so inextricably tied together.

CRATER LAKE RIM AND MOUNT SHASTA

Seen from the rim of Crater Lake, Mount Shasta lies on the horizon, a hundred miles away in California. At 14,162 feet, it's the second-highest of all Cascade peaks, outdone only by Mount Rainier in Washington.

With the sources of the Rogue, Klamath, and Umpqua Rivers surrounding Crater Lake, and with refuges of ancient forest still scattered at the periphery of the national park, Oregon conservationists have supported the designation of a Greater Mount Mazama National Park to fully protect the whole ecosystem that encircles this wondrous lake.

WHITEBARK PINE

Excelling as one of the highest-elevation trees in America, the whitebark pine grows on the leanest and stormiest sites. Rarely found west of the Cascade crest, these small and wind-twisted pines literally define timberline, which often occurs at about 6,500 feet in the Oregon Cascades.

This tree enjoys an unusual symbiotic relationship with the Clark's nutcracker, a boisterous black-and-white bird often seen in the highcountry. Seeds of the whitebark lack membranous wings that allow other pine seeds to scatter on the wind. But making up for that handicap, whitebark seeds are attractive to birds because they offer rich oils and proteins. The nutcrackers industriously collect the seeds, eating some but burying thousands in multiple caches up to fourteen miles apart. While the nutcrackers retrieve many seeds throughout the year, they store two or three times as many as they can eat, effectively planting them far and wide. Trouble for the pines thus means trouble for the nutcrackers, and vice versa, an example of the connectedness of all things in the natural world.

ABOVE: MORNING LIGHT ILLUMINES CALIFORNIA'S MOUNT SHASTA, 100 MILES SOUTH FROM THE RIM OF CRATER LAKE.

FACING PAGE: THIS WHITEBARK PINE HAS STOOD FOR CENTURIES AT THE WEST RIM OF CRATER LAKE.

LICHEN ON VINE
MAPLE BRANCHES

A lichen called witch's hair (*Alectoria sarmentosa*) hangs from the branches of this vine maple in a Cascade forest. The large quantities of mosses, lichens, and fungi that flourish on the maples and in the root zones of northwestern conifers do not harm the trees but rather support them in essential ways. As they cling to branches, lichens rake moisture out of the persistent fog and accumulate it until water drips down into the root zone of the trees. Underground fungi produce chemicals used by the host tree to ward off pests and also to process nutrients that enhance growth and survival of the tree. The health of the forest thus depends on a vibrant crop of primitive plants and microorganisms, which in turn require clean air and healthy soil that's not poisoned by herbicides or eroded by careless logging.

UPPER ROGUE RIVER

The Rogue River begins at Boundary Springs, just northwest of Crater Lake, with flows that seep from the caldera itself. Then the river plunges through a gallery of fractured basalt, the entire flow at one point disappearing underground. Hissing and blowing cold air out of cracks in the rock, the Rogue courses through hollow tubes in the lava, then fizzes back up to the surface and resumes its Pacific-bound path. Trails parallel the upper river through old-growth stands of fir and pine, and in autumn through the flaming red of dogwood, the orange of vine maple, and the sunny yellow of willows. With forty-three miles of the upper river protected in the National Wild and Scenic Rivers System, the Rogue is a refuge for elk, fishers, gray foxes, ringtail cats, and cutthroat trout. The national river designation banned a hydroelectric dam once proposed at the geologically unique Natural Bridge. Below the town of Grants Pass, a lower section of the 210-mile Rogue includes one of the most sought-after whitewater trips in the West.

LICHENS DRAPE THE BRANCHES OF A VINE MAPLE IN THE ROGUE RIVER NATIONAL FOREST.

A pioneering willow tree holds its own along the basalt banks of the upper Rogue.

UPPER KLAMATH LAKE

The largest lake in Oregon, Klamath stretches for twenty-three miles along the eastern foot of the Cascades. With its upper end designated as one of the nation's first national wildlife refuges, Klamath hosts some of America's largest gatherings of waterfowl, the largest wintering group of bald eagles in the lower forty-eight states, and hundreds of other species of migrating birds. Twenty-five kinds of fish are found here, eight of them existing nowhere else.

While the lake's primary source is the Williamson River, its outlet becomes the Klamath River, the third-largest waterway on the West Coast south of Canada as it flows 263 miles to the ocean. Only the Columbia and Sacramento River systems historically supported more salmon and steelhead. These fish once thrived in the upper Klamath but are now extinct above Iron Gate Dam near the California border. Downstream, salmon still return to spawn but are limited by low flows, pollution, and high temperatures owing to the water's use and reuse for farming. As a result, a whole fishing industry off the West Coast has been lost, including 6,870 jobs and the principal occupation of three whole tribes of Indians.

Rich as the Klamath basin is for birdlife in Oregon, it's only a shadow of its earlier self. During World War I the Department of the Interior yielded to local ranchers' wishes to drain part of the lake for cattle pasture and farmland. Nearby Tule Lake and Lower Klamath Marshes were likewise drained. Historic migrations of 6 million birds have dropped to 2 or 3 million, and 90 percent of the wetlands rimming the lake have been drained or filled while the federal dams delivered water at a $20 million annual subsidy to agriculture. One of many results, the shortnose sucker—once an important food fish for Indians—is almost extinct.

In summer 2001 the Endangered Species Act and other laws required the federal Bureau of Reclamation to leave minimal flows in the river for fish and wildlife, triggering intense controversy in the

ASPEN AND COTTONWOOD TRUNKS ARMOR THE SHORELINE OF
UPPER KLAMATH LAKE AT SHOALWATER BAY.

upper basin. In 2002 the Bush administration reinstated diversions to the farmers, and then 30,000 adult salmon died owing to low flows in the river downstream. This was one of the worst fish kills in the history of the West. Meanwhile upstream, The Nature Conservancy has negotiated with landowners since 1996 and pieced together a program for restoring habitat on the delta of the Williamson River— a critical site for saving the life of this great lake.

MOUNT MCLOUGHLIN

As the southernmost high peak in Oregon's Cascades, Mount McLoughlin rises to 9,495 feet. Lacquered with the snows of winter, the nearly perfect cone overlooks Klamath Lake. Without the deep cavities of erosion that surround older volcanic peaks, McLoughlin's mostly conical shape reveals its youth and may signal that this volcano is still active. The Cascade Mountains are a great masterpiece still in progress.

STEEPED IN CONTROVERSY OVER WHETHER WATER SHOULD BE USED FOR IRRIGATION OR LEFT IN THE RIVER SO THAT SALMON AND OTHER NATIVE LIFE CAN SURVIVE, THE KLAMATH BASIN GLOWS BENEATH THE SNOWY SUMMIT OF MOUNT MCLOUGHLIN.

CHAPTER 4

CANYONS AND GRASSLANDS

The Elegance of a Lonely Land

In eastern Oregon, mountains and drylands stretch as far as the eye can see and then they stretch beyond—far beyond. Although it encompasses nearly two-thirds of the state, Oregon east of the Cascades is unknown to many people, its views unexpected. Back on the west side, the land is green and abundant with life, but here to the east the arid plateaus and lonely mountaintops are the counterpoint. While the west side sees 40 to 200 inches of rainfall, the east side gets only 10 to 25 inches, and the difference makes for a whole other world.

This is no longer the West Coast but rather the American West, a place of sunshine and blue skies, big spaces, dusty dirt roads, and echoing dry canyons where hawks soar overhead and where stepping on a rattlesnake is not out of the question. Cowboys replace the lumberjacks of western Oregon, and its cities are not replaced at all.

Though aridity unifies the land beyond the Cascades, eastern Oregon still has distinctive regions. The south-central reaches are part of the Great Basin—a desert vastness of sagebrush punctuated by mountains that feed streams into landlocked lakes. Similarly dry but with watercourses that eventually find their way to the ocean, southeastern Oregon is cut by the Malheur River and also by the Owyhee, which winds from juniper-clad uplands and disappears into scoriaceous slits between dark, rocky walls that speak of isolation and mystery. In the central and northern reaches, ranges including the Ochoco, Aldrich, Strawberry, Blue, and Wallowa are often lumped together as the Blue Mountains. This partly forested terrain rises up to granite summits, dips down to swales and valleys, and is encircled by volcanic plateaus of blackened lava. To the north lies the Columbia Plateau with fertile but dry, windblown soil called loess.

Here in eastern Oregon, plains of sage and juniper roll out like a whiskered land to the sunset. Gorges of disorienting depth cut across the ground as if a monstrous claw had raked the earth. Ridge tops edge the horizon and gray-green mountains ramp upward in pine-clad slopes to snowfields that drift deep but then melt in a blister of summer sun. Finally, our tour of Oregon ends in the glorious, furious, undebatably awesome spectacle of Hells Canyon, where the Snake River scribes the boundary with Idaho.

STEENS MOUNTAIN, A HIGHLIGHT OF EASTERN OREGON, RISES ABOVE KIGER CREEK GORGE.

LAKE BED PLAYA

Climate counts—a fact abundantly evident at the Alvord Desert beneath the high rise of Steens Mountain. All the wet cloud masses that blow-in off the Pacific, soaking the Coast Range from November through May and dumping foot upon foot of snow on the Cascades, become just a whiff of desiccating wind here in eastern Oregon. The place, however, has high mountains of its own, and each time the prevailing winds are pushed upslope again, the same process of condensation is reenacted, causing rain or snow to drop on the heights of Hart Mountain, Steens Mountain, the Blue Mountains, and the enchanting Wallowas. Likewise, a rain shadow is repeated on the downwind or eastern sides of each of those ranges, and drylands are the result.

Here at the Alvord Desert, in the sunset-shadow of Steens Mountain, aridity is extreme. Sand dunes and hot springs bring variety to this austere land.

In a place like this, the silence of the desert can be overwhelming. We expect quietness in small and protected spaces, but in terrain that's open out to the distant curvature of the earth, the quiet is startling and profound. Desert air is hot by day, cold by night, sharp and abrasive all the time. One could never anticipate a place more opposite from the surf at Ecola or the mossy forest along the Elk River. Yet all of this is Oregon.

ASPENS GRACE THE FLANKS OF STEENS MOUNTAIN.

A LAKE-BED PLAYA CRACKS IN THE SUMMER SUN AT THE ALVORD DESERT.

John Day Fossil Beds

Buried in volcanic ash 16 to 25 million years ago, the skeletons of saber-toothed tigers, three-toed horses, and other long-extinct fauna have been unearthed at the John Day Fossil Beds. Here ancient lava flows dammed many streams, and then further volcanic fireworks threw darkening quantities of ash into the skies. Settling and washing into the dammed-up lakes, this rhyolite ash made just the sticky medium needed for perfect imprints of leaves, bones, and whole fossilized skeletons. Today we can see the record of oreodonts—stocky creatures that looked like sheep. Paleontologists have uncovered little cousins of the hippo right here in Oregon. Back when the climate was wetter, even a hornless rhinoceros grunted his way across prehistoric plains.

The Zumwalt Prairie Preserve

Ranchers pioneered eastern Oregon after the fertile spreads in the farming-friendly Willamette Valley were taken. The dry, demanding land on the east side of the Cascades posed a hard life for people and livestock alike, and many of the homesteads so hopefully settled were later abandoned.

Though green here in the brief springtime, the grasses of eastern Oregon dry up in summer to a static sea of golden brown. In the temperate eastern states, one acre can satisfy a cow and calf, and you often see cows contented enough to sit down in their pasture. But here in the arid West, each cow needs 50, 100, or even 200 acres of forage, and you almost never see cows sitting down—the pickings are so lean that a large animal has to be eating all the time.

Now owned by The Nature Conservancy, the Zumwalt Prairie Preserve in northeastern Oregon is one of the finest locations where bunchgrasses still thrive. These hearty natives mix with a host of wildflowers, including paintbrush, balsamroot, and brodiaea in one of the rarest ecosystems left in Oregon and the West. Hillsides dip steeply into the canyon of the Imnaha River—one of the outstanding tributaries to the Snake and Columbia Rivers.

Blue-green claystone weathers through time in the Blue Basin amphitheater of John Day Fossil Beds National Monument, Sheep Rock Unit.

THE NATURE CONSERVANCY HAS PROTECTED THE ZUMWALT PRAIRIE AT HUBBARD RANCH IN THE WALLOWA MOUNTAINS.

ZUMWALT PRAIRIE DIPS DOWN INTO THE SPECTACULAR IMNAHA RIVER CANYON.

JOHN DAY RIVER

The John Day River begins in the conifer-shaded Blue Mountains and passes beneath chocolate brown hills and through fractured basalt canyons to the Columbia.

One of the longest mostly free-flowing rivers in the West, the main stem flows for 243 miles with no major dams. Only the lower 12 miles are impounded by The Dalles Dam on the Columbia. The North, South, and Middle Forks likewise flow freely over rapids and from watersheds covered by trees and grass. With some of the largest uncut forests in eastern Oregon, it's no coincidence that the North Fork supports one of the largest populations of spring chinook salmon and summer steelhead in the Columbia River basin.

The John Day is also the only major river in Oregon without hatchery-planted fish. Though the intent of hatcheries is to increase numbers of fish, most scientists now recognize that they actually depress native or wild fish populations. Lacking both hatcheries and dams, the John Day figures prominently in efforts to protect and restore salmon and steelhead in the Columbia basin.

THE PAINTED HILLS

Unusual, rare, and endangered desert plants still survive in remote reaches of the John Day basin. Bee-plant has pink or yellow blooms and grows on dry slopes. Though it doesn't smell appetizing, this plant is said to have saved Indians from starvation. Chaenactis, or false-yarrow, produces white flowers highly regarded by Indians for use as poultices to reduce inflammation; the Paiute name for this plant means "swelling medicine." A tea was also applied to chapped hands, bee stings, and snake bites. Both these plants hint at the richness of the native flora that once covered the hills of eastern Oregon.

HART MOUNTAIN

Ratcheted skyward by earthquakes, Hart Mountain veers up from the desert. While the flats below host dryland plants such as Wyoming sagebrush, and pond into wetlands formed by snowmelt, the upper slopes are cloaked with mountain mahogany, western juniper, and even aspen. In 1936, to protect pronghorn, which thrive on sage-brush, local residents pushed for the establishment of the Hart Mountain National Antelope Refuge. At that time half of Oregon's 2,000 pronghorn (often called antelope) lived in the area. Bighorn sheep, which had already been driven to extinction locally through overhunting and diseases spread by domestic sheep, were reintroduced in 1956. Both these impressive wild ungulates now graze on the mountain's flanks.

BUILDINGS OF THE HISTORIC CANT RANCH CAN STILL BE SEEN IN JOHN DAY FOSSIL BEDS NATIONAL MONUMENT.

Steep parts of Hart Mountain were protected in the wildlife refuge, but dozens of homesteads already established made it difficult for refuge managers to allow naturally occurring fires—important to the succession and survival of native plants and wildlife forage. In order to ranch here, cattlemen had also diverted springs and creeks or fenced them off for cattle, eliminating fish and wildlife.

Recognizing the needs of the refuge, The Nature Conservancy has bought 10,000 acres from willing sellers to build a more complete preserve.

THE JOHN DAY RIVER—ONE OF THE MOST CRITICAL SALMON STREAMS REMAINING—FLOWS THROUGH THE
SHEEP ROCK UNIT OF JOHN DAY FOSSIL BEDS NATIONAL MONUMENT.

THE PAINTED HILLS ROLL ACROSS JOHN DAY FOSSIL BEDS NATIONAL MONUMENT.

As part of the HART MOUNTAIN NATIONAL ANTELOPE REFUGE, POKER JIM RIDGE rises above WARNER VALLEY wetlands.

NATIVE GRASSES SURVIVE ON THE PROTECTED SLOPES OF HART MOUNTAIN.

BUNCHGRASSES

Bunchgrasses, such as these tufted clumps on the rocky slopes of Hart Mountain, once graced eastern Oregon in vast sweeps of grass from the foot of the Cascades to the Snake River. Being deep-rooted, the bunchgrasses can survive the intense heat and dryness of summer. Tapping underground water supplies, they remain green through much of the year—an ideal source of food for deer, elk, and other animals.

Unfortunately the bunchgrasses are also a favorite food of cows, and when grazed repeatedly, the native grasses died because their leaves could no longer support vibrant root stalks. Taking their place, shallow-rooted annual grasses were introduced from old-world locations. Aggressive by any standards in the plant world, these grasses sprout quickly, sucking up the springtime water and throwing down a prodigious crop of seeds before other plants can make a start. Dying out by early summer, the annual grasses offer little food value compared to what the native grasses once provided for wildlife and cattle. Further clinching their grip on the land, cheatgrass and some other introduced weeds do well when burned. Once ensconced, they become dominant. Statewide more than 80 percent of the native grasslands have been overrun by noxious invaders, making bunchgrass refuges like this one on Hart Mountain especially valuable.

RABBIT BRUSH CATCHES EVENING LIGHT AT THE BUENA VISTA PONDS OF MALHEUR NATIONAL WILDLIFE REFUGE.

MALHEUR NATIONAL WILDLIFE REFUGE

It may seem axiomatic that rivers flow to the sea, but the runoff from Steens Mountain, Hart Mountain, and the other peaks of south-central Oregon does not flow to any ocean. Rather, it flows to low lakes completely surrounded by higher ground and then evaporates. The outcome isn't the "dead sea" that one might expect. Instead the lakes and wetlands that result are among the most critical in the interior West for waterfowl and migratory birds. Malheur Lake is the largest natural freshwater marsh west of the Mississippi. Ponded waters here, along with dozens of lakes and wetlands beneath Hart Mountain, the Abert Rim, and Diablo Peak, are vital to the life of south-central Oregon.

Tundra swans, pintail ducks, sandhill cranes, and snow geese arrive in February. Cranes nest in April, and the springtime also brings curlews, avocets, and stilts. Around the margins of the wetlands, salt-tolerant shrubs such as winterfat, saltsage, and greasewood do well, accompanied by whole suites of reptiles and small mammals. Malheur's open-air aviary is the last thing one might expect to find in the harsh desert, but nature is full of surprises, and because of water flowing down from the mountains, life persists here.

ASPEN TREES

In the midst of drylands, Steens Mountain rose high enough, wet enough, and cold enough to spawn glaciers during the last ice age. In five places carved by these glaciers, U-shaped valleys flame in autumn with the brilliant foliage of quaking aspen. This grove lies along the Donner und Blitzen River, one of Oregon's National Wild and Scenic Rivers.

Growing primarily from shoots sprouting from the roots, all the aspens in a particular clump are genetically the same, originating from one parent rootstock. The tree is relished by porcupines in winter and by elk that chew its tender bark. It's also a favorite food of the beaver. Wildfires are important to the aspens' long-term health, because in many areas Engelmann spruce tend to grow beneath the pioneering deciduous trees and eventually shade them out. But after fire, the aspen sprout vigorously.

ASPEN COLOR THE FLOOR OF FISH CREEK CANYON WHERE
THE DONNER UND BLITZEN RIVER FLOWS DOWN
FROM STEENS MOUNTAIN.

STEENS MOUNTAIN

Steep sided, plateau-topped Steens Mountain rises to 9,773 feet and sweeps boldly north-south for fifty miles. As the highest mountain in southern Oregon, Steens' amalgam of basalt, andesite, and crystalline rocks has been pushed up by earthquakes over the course of the last 7 million years.

A vertical mile above the Alvord Desert, the summit of Steens Mountain receives forty inches of precipitation a year, while the desert straight below gets a meager seven inches. Reflecting the change in elevation, one distinctive zone of life succeeds another as you rise up the flanks by trail or by road. At lower elevations, the kangaroo rat, burrowing owl, and rare kit fox can be found. Above 5,000 feet, pronghorns browse, jackrabbits dart in the brush, and rattlesnakes curl under rocks. At the higher elevations, aspen rustle on the slightest breeze and a herd of 200 bighorn sheep graze. In the springtime, snowmelt rips down the staircase streams of 2,000-foot-deep canyons.

ABOVE: THE JAGGED RIDGES OF STEENS MOUNTAIN'S EAST RIM DROP DOWN TO THE ALVORD DESERT.

RIGHT: CLOUDS SWIRL AT THE SUMMIT OF STEENS MOUNTAIN'S EAST RIM.

ALVORD DESERT

A study in contrasts, the Alvord Desert bakes in the lowlands beneath the face of Steens Mountain. Hot springs bubble up along the fault lines that allow water to rise from the boiling inner recesses of the earth.

Hot Lake, heated by a geothermal spring, is full of borax, which was mined here from 1898 to 1907. Chinese laborers gleaned the salty crusts off the ground and then boiled them to extract the well-known cleansing agent, also used in blowing glass, making porcelain, and tanning hides.

Several basins here become vernal pools that later evaporate in the searing heat of summer. After the rains of autumn begin, spadefoot toads spring to life from muddy underground burrows where they had taken cover and estivated during the long siege of drought.

WETLANDS AND
BUCKSKIN MOUNTAIN

The Borax wetlands are just a vestige of the 500-square-mile lake that covered the Alvord lowlands when the glaciers melted 10,000 to 40,000 years ago. Some of the same species that survive today had their beginnings in that massive lake and became isolated as it dried up.

An unrepeated mix of plants and animals has evolved in this unusual area including a two-inch-long endangered fish, the Borax Lake chub. Five species of arthropods previously unknown to science were discovered here, along with two cave-dwelling invertebrates found nowhere else.

ABOVE: BUCKSKIN MOUNTAIN RISES BEYOND THE PROTECTED WETLANDS
OF THE ALVORD DESERT.

FACING PAGE: THE ALVORD DESERT STRETCHES OUT TOWARD STEENS MOUNTAIN.

LESLIE GULCH

Leading down into the Owyhee River canyon, Leslie Gulch presents a showcase of badlands and sky-pointing pinnacles. This canyon is part of the 70 percent of southeast Oregon owned by the American public and overseen by the federal Bureau of Land Management.

EAGLE CAP PEAK AND MIRROR LAKE

Completely different from anything else in the entire Northwest, the Wallowa Range is like an outlier of the Rocky Mountains. High granite peaks rise above painted meadows of wildflowers, canyons misted by waterfalls, and forests of sweetly resinous pine and fir. Here is Oregon's largest tract of contiguous alpine terrain, with seventeen peaks over 9,000 feet high. Eagle Cap, a granite giant at 9,595 feet, looks down on everything around it.

A seismic uplift of 5,000 feet heaved the Wallowas' thick slabs of granite into place. Meanwhile, overlying lava eroded off the top to expose the gleaming whitish rock underneath. Glaciers gouged out cirque basins at high elevations and carved U-shaped valleys leading down to rivers. Ice whittled rocky faces, plucked boulders from the headwalls of the peaks, and pushed soil, stones, and broken bedrock and deposited them as moraines of rocky rubble that dammed streams and created fifty-eight mountain lakes. This handiwork can be seen in one eyeful at Mirror Lake.

ABOVE: GLACIERS POLISHED THESE ROCKS ABOVE MIRROR LAKE.

FACING PAGE: IN SOUTHEASTERN OREGON, VOLCANIC TUFF HAS HARDENED INTO HONEYCOMBED CLIFFS AT LESLIE GULCH IN THE OWYHEE RIVER BASIN.

OVERLEAF: WILDERNESS DESIGNATION PROTECTS MIRROR LAKE IN THE WALLOWA-WHITMAN NATIONAL FOREST.

In far eastern Oregon—as far as you can get in this state from the Pacific Ocean—I have another favorite place. After climbing for hours across grassy slopes and through scattered groves of ponderosa pine, I sit on high, forested slopes above the great canyon of the Snake River. Deeper than any other canyon in America except for the Kings River Canyon of California, Hells Canyon separates Oregon from Idaho and soars from a searing rockbound desert at its base to a cool and breezy forest at its rim.

From my overlook I can reflect on the many faces of this land. As the Columbia's largest tributary, the Snake flows for 1,059 miles from its source in Yellowstone National Park and then across the agricultural flats of southern Idaho where the entire river is diverted for farming and hydropower. Yet it springs back to life here at the border of Idaho and Oregon for one final fling through the greatest of its canyons, 5,000 feet below the perch where I rest. Like the other waters of Oregon flowing from other ranges of mountains, this river swirls through the ages, its life a source of hope and satisfaction for anyone willing to sit and listen to the currents.

The runoff of snowmelt and groundwater is bound for the ocean, down to where our tour of Oregon began—on a beach—a beach whose very own sand may have come from some long-forgotten flood of the Snake River.

CONIFEROUS FORESTS PATTERN THE LAND AT THE WESTERN RIM OF HELLS CANYON.

CHAPTER 5

OREGON

Home for the Generations to Come

In this book celebrating the land and life of Oregon, it's no coincidence that nearly all of the photos were taken in places that are publicly owned and protected as wilderness areas, state parks, national monuments, wildlife refuges, national wild and scenic rivers, and one national park. These are the lands where nature is allowed to thrive and where the beauty regarded as quintessentially Oregon can still be found. Yet, statewide, only 10 percent of the land is actually safeguarded in these kinds of reserves.

Outside these reserves, enormous changes have been wrought on the earth and water, and many more changes are in store. Of course there are beautiful places beyond the protected boundaries— much of Oregon is stewarded well by many owners. But outside the reserves one also finds a multitude of clear-cut forests, overgrazed plains, bulldozed riverfronts, coastlines cluttered with condominiums, and commercialized savanna where you might find one lonely oak tree spared at the center of a sprawling parking lot or mall.

Like elsewhere, here the world of nature and the world of vastly altered nature both exist. But in Oregon they both exist very close to each other. Traveling up and down the seashore and across the ridges and valleys, I am reminded of this closeness again and again. For example, from the top of Cascade Head, the extravagance of the Pacific coast lays below me in stands of aged forest, in the stately procession of sea stacks, in the great swell of surf. But just inland, a checkerboard of clear-cuts monopolizes the view. In the otherwise-

heavenly valley of the Elk River, a hideous, thorny, exotic shrub called gorse has grown in the wake of soil disturbance associated with logging, and it tyrannically displaces all native vegetation and wildlife.

Likewise, from the top of Mount Tabor in Portland, the snow-bound visage of Mount Hood rises high to the east, but traffic and sprawl smoke out from the city to the suburbs. From Steens Mountain, the wildness of rock and aspen glide down the slopes, but on the flats below, a century of grazing has left an infusion of Eurasian cheatgrass and prickly weeds taking the place of nutritious bunchgrasses that once stretched as far as the eye could see and nourished a Serengeti of antelope, deer, elk, and bighorn sheep.

From each of these views and a thousand more, you can inhale the breath of natural abundance so elegantly recorded in the photos of this book, and you can also see the effects of nearly 200 years of settlement. Since the days of the Oregon Trail, white settlers have been intent on using the land. And much of what we've done has eliminated the finest blessings our ancestors ever enjoyed—an inheritance as basic as clean water, fertile soil, free food in the form of fish, and room to roam or escape the din of modern-day traffic. Yet increasing pressures have made many Oregonians aware of what's at stake, and many have thus embraced an ethic of stewardship.

The photographs here show dozens of real and specific places that anyone can go and see, but they also represent the rest of Oregon not shown in these images, both inside and outside nature's reserves.

ONE OF THE FINEST STREAMS OF THE NORTHWEST, THE UPPER ROGUE NEAR UNION CREEK IS PROTECTED
AS A NATIONAL WILD AND SCENIC RIVER.

The crystal-clear waters of Silver Creek might well stand for all waters as they once flowed throughout the state's 114,500 miles of rivers and streams. A girthy pair of ponderosa pines signifies the old-growth forests that once blanketed so much of the Northwest on both sides of the Cascades. The photos might be thought of as symbols of a well-tended Oregon. Parts of this remain. And much can be restored.

Here are some reasons why protection and restoration efforts have caught the attention of many Oregonians. For starters, 50,000 new residents have recently been added to the state per year, each bringing his or her expectation of quality, his or her weight of occupation to the land and its limited resources. In the 1990s the Beaver State's growth rate was two times the national average. Each year, farm and forest acreage equal to the city of Medford was turned into urban and rural sprawl; in just a decade, that totals twice the size of Portland. Another million people were projected for the next twenty years, inevitably causing Oregon to look more like the unsatisfying places that the newcomers so deliberately left behind.

Next, consider the salmon. If there was ever a living emblem of northwestern life, this is it—a fish that runs deep in the mythology, history, economy, sport life, and common consciousness of so many Oregonians. But nearly all native salmon stocks are in radical decline and most are listed as endangered or threatened. Combined coho salmon populations plummeted from 1.5 million historically to a mere 50,000 in the late 1990s. Many salmon runs have already gone extinct. It should be no surprise that in a period when nine-tenths of the forests were cut down, these fish declined 97 percent; when the forests were cut, the streams became silted and damaged, the spawning beds destroyed.

And we're talking more than fish here. When the salmon go down the road to oblivion, a whole Noah's Ark of other creatures goes with them. Not only do some forty-three kinds of mammals and birds feed directly on the keystone salmon, but virtually all life along the rivers depends to some degree on the salmon's role in the food and carbon cycles. This is because the fish retrieve nutrients from the sea and redistribute them at the headwaters of every accessible stream when they spawn and die. As the fish become recycled into the water and streamside soils, their nutrients account for many of the life-giving elements in floodplain vegetation, local insect populations, and other building blocks of great ecosystems. Whatever happens to the salmon will tell much about the quality of life that people and all creatures will enjoy in the years ahead. Nothing less than the nature of Oregon is at stake.

In addition to the salmon, 45 percent of the state's freshwater fish are at risk of being endangered. In this regard, Oregon is the fifth-worst state in the nation. Water pollution is one reason; according to state data, more than two-thirds of the streams fail to meet water quality standards.

Terrestrial ecosystems are in deep trouble as well. Only 10 percent of the old-growth forests are left. Five percent of the oak woodlands remain. Two percent of the sagebrush-bunchgrass ecosystem is protected. A mere 1 percent of the Willamette Valley native grasslands can be found, no matter how hard one looks for them. Because of lost habitat statewide, biologists now regard 200 species of plants and animals as highly vulnerable to being snuffed out entirely. Forever.

These landscapes are not just important to the native life of Oregon but to the production and maintenance of goods and services necessary to the lives and future of all people in the state. Without soil we cannot grow food or trees, but soil erosion from agricultural land totaled nearly 12 million tons in the 1990s, a rate considered excessive. Pollution of streams means that our drinking water will be ruined. Damage to watersheds means that flood costs will rise. Without healthy ecosystems, we will lack healthy and productive forests, range, farmland, water, and even air to breathe.

Many of the most pressing needs for land conservation lie in the lowlands of the state—the river valleys, wetlands, and grasslands. Half of these habitats have already been converted to agriculture, suburbs, and exotic weeds, with the losses reaching 98 percent in the most populated and agricultural regions. When such grim statistics are tabulated, it's clear that the proverbial glass of optimism is neither half empty nor half full in the figurative sense, but rather mostly empty in a purely factual sense—something that's difficult for an informed person to deny or ignore.

Yet, like this book, I prefer to dwell on what's left and to celebrate it with great enthusiasm. If we don't nurture strong feelings about the land—if we don't enjoy it and love it—we lose our connection to the earth altogether. Then, as if gravity had disappeared, we all float free of our cultural, historical, and ecological moorings—free of all support and safety that the earth had provided.

Striving to stay connected, I always remind myself that Oregon is one of a kind—still a land of exquisite beauty. Compared to most other states, nature survives here in large pieces. Where else can one find forest-blanketed mountains slanting into the Pacific like they do at Oswald West State Park? Where else do rivers like the North Umpqua course down from highcountry, through deep woods, and then out to sea where the salmon wait for the opportune moment to fin their way back upstream to spawn? Where else do volcanic peaks reach for the sky and catch enough snow to keep glaciers alive this far south? With the state parks of the Pacific edge, the scenic wonderland of the Columbia Gorge, the ancient forests of the Cascades, and the austere wilds of the deserts, Oregon's natural endowment remains a centerpiece to everyone who lives here and everyone who comes to visit.

Inspired by magnificent places, many citizens have acted with

Dawn breaks at old rock cairns in Zumwalt Prairie, the Wallowa Mountains in the background.

YAQUINA HEAD BREAKS THE WAVES OF THE PACIFIC.

courage and vigilance to protect what remains. Thanks to Governor Oswald West in 1913, the beaches of Oregon are not fenced-off by "private property" and "members only" signs, but rather owned by the state and available for use by everyone. If it weren't for Governor West, the legislature in Salem would have sold off these tidal lands for the kind of development now seen at beaches in many other states—posted, gated, monitored by electronic surveillance, and policed by private security forces. In 1967 the advocates of public access got another boost when Oregon's famed "Beach Bill" made the dry-sand areas above high tide available to the public as well, allowing people to walk up and down the beaches and preventing commercialization from pressing in so closely on the beauties and fearsome hazards of the sea.

Back in 1938, schoolchildren demonstrated in the streets with placards that said, "The youth of Portland demand clean rivers." From the governors of both parties to those spunky little kids a whole lifetime ago, thousands of Oregonians have been involved in countless ways to safeguard this land.

Consider for a moment two men who are scarcely known but are heroes nonetheless: Bob Potter and Bob Pierce. River runners in the 1960s, Potter rowed his drift boat and Pierce rowed his raft on the Rogue and the Sandy, the Deschutes and the McKenzie. They were just like other Oregonians who loved the outdoors. But more perceptive than most, they took careful note of all they saw. And what they saw was a lot of change—not only from pollution but also from encroaching homesites and other development. They saw the advance of sprawl and the plans for unneeded dams that would permanently flood streams as gem-like as the Illinois and Snake, the Santiam and Applegate. Potter worked at the harbor in Portland; Pierce designed publications for the city's art museum. Neither got paid to do what they knew was most important, but each used his substantial talent to launch a state scenic rivers program. They collected thousands of signatures for a ballot initiative and ultimately got a law passed to set up a system of state-protected rivers. They guided their streams through a shooting gallery of dam proposals and past the worst of the bulldozer threats. Their commitment and success were repeated by others in the following decades.

In the 1970s Oregon was the first state to adopt a law calling for urban-growth boundaries. The law encourages development inside the boundaries and discourages it outside of them. This forward thinking policy enhanced the economies of cities and towns while protecting farmland for farming, forests for forestry, and open spaces for the good of all people as well as for the natural systems that make life not only pleasant but possible. This land-use law remains the single most important factor in keeping Oregon a desirable, economic, and beautiful place to live.

In the 1980s attention turned to the mountains when an eclectic cadre of Oregonians recognized that few of the old-growth forests remained. They set about protecting all they could through path-breaking scientific studies, the recharting of Forest Service policy, court cases, sit-down protests, and a persistent appeal to citizens to recognize the forests' importance to all life. Rising out of those efforts, the Northwest Forest Plan adopted by the Clinton administration set aside much of the surviving old-growth. Reserves now total two-thirds of the federally owned forest land of the western Cascades, some of it completely protected and some of it open to limited logging. Although criticized on one side for saving too much because marketable timber was locked up, and criticized on the other side because 90 percent of the old forest had already been cut and the entire 10 percent left didn't seem like too much to spare at that point, the plan clearly set aside more ancient forest than ever before.

In the 1990s and continuing into the twenty-first century, the endangered status of the salmon and steelhead brought legions of other citizens together for better care of our land. More than just a question of fish, more than just a question of rivers, the fate of these creatures and the streams they inhabit says a great deal about how we treat our entire landscape, from logging and grazing to backyard septic tanks and the megawatt-spinning dams on the Columbia. To consider the fate of the salmon, you have to consider everything that the fish and their rivers touch.

The rivers, in fact, are the report cards on all that we do to the land. If farms or ranches or shopping centers leave soil exposed, it washes off into the streams and clogs the fishes' spawning beds. If clear-cuts or seas of sun-baked asphalt cause runoff to be heated—and they do—then the fish will die. If dams block the way to and from headwater homes, entire runs go extinct.

Commercial fishermen at every port up and down the coast, resort owners up and down every river, sport anglers from all over the nation, Indian tribes from all over the Northwest, small-town businessmen, river conservationists, and local residents of every stripe have rallied to bring the salmon back by improving the streams. Just one of hundreds of Oregonians pressing for reform, Gayle Killam of River Network trains local activists in the use of the federal Clean Water Act, which includes provisions for eliminating and preventing pollution everywhere. While Bob Potter and Bob Pierce had worked to protect a select group of the state's best rivers, people like Gayle Killam now strive to see that we respect every stream, large and small.

For years a fisherman and medical doctor, John Kitzhaber understood the importance of good land and clean water to both wildlife and people, and he won election as governor with campaign promises to protect the health of his state. Yet this proved to be quite a challenge when reactionary legislators—many of them bought and paid for by powerful economic interests—passed dozens of bills to gut the environmental laws so painfully enacted over the previous thirty years. Proposals were advanced to usurp public lands so that the state could sell off every Oregonian's birthright in national forests to private developers. In one year alone Kitzhaber vetoed forty bills that would have weakened or eliminated Oregon's legacy of protection. In 1999, 130 bills were introduced to cripple a few laws that curb sprawl. The state's famed land-use statute became the target of a contingent seeking to topple local democratic control by giving developers free reign over the fate of whole communities.

Most of the worst proposals were fended off, though the threats continue and the only thing stopping the tide of loss is the action of people who care about the land. From Governor West to Governor Kitzhaber, from Bob Potter to Gayle Killam, Oregonians have worked tirelessly to protect a place they know is essential. The Oregon Natural Resources Council, Oregon Environmental Council, 1000 Friends of Oregon, Save Our Wild Salmon Coalition, The Nature Conservancy, Oregon Trout, Friends of the Columbia River Gorge, and Portland Audubon Society are just a few among dozens of groups trying to safeguard the future for us all.

Still a teenager back in 1967, I puffed my way up the South Sister, a 10,358-foot mountain west of Bend. From down below, the big rounded dome had caught my eye with its shine of snow and its rusty streaks of pumice melted out by summer sun. I hustled up a trail along a drinkable stream, walked through whole meadows splayed with the blue of gentian and lupine, entered the miniature forest of whitebark pine, and finally strided up the cindered slopes of loose rock and onto deep drifts of snow. At the top, an azure pool of water, half frozen, filled the once-boiling crater. I walked around the volcano's rim to the wind-blasted summit and paused there with the whole mountain underfoot.

All Oregon lay stretched-out below. The wind had come directly from the Pacific and still felt moist as it whisked over the highcountry before beginning its warm, dry descent down the east face of the Cascades. In its billowing breath across the land, the wind crossed all the varied elements of the state, Pacific Ocean to Rocky Mountain fringe. Mosaics of pine, fir, and cedar swept down from timberline into one of the world's greatest conifer forests blanketing the west side of the mountains. Multiple rivers knifed into the land, each a miniature Columbia Gorge. The drylands of the east rolled out into miles and miles that didn't end until their plunge into the great canyon of the Snake River, far, far out of sight.

The times have changed since I first stood there on the summit of the South Sister and looked out across Oregon. Back then the towns were small, the cities not congested with traffic. Pulp mills polluted the Willamette River quite heavily, but the computer industry hadn't yet arrived. Logging seemed to be a way of life, but the pace of clear-cutting hadn't yet reached the rapacious level it would during the timber boom of the 1980s. The mills of the Northwest were not yet automated and so they employed many more men—30,000 more than they later did, even when more timber was being cut. There was still a powerful and proud sense that Oregon was a place apart. And there were strong sentiments to keep it that way. In 1970 Governor Tom McCall said, "We must first and foremost cherish the place. All other good things will follow if we recognize the special beauty of Oregon . . . if we revere the magic . . . if we protect the quality."

The times have changed, yet much of the view from the South Sister still looks the same, the mountains still intact, the desert still stretching far away beyond the reach of modern sprawl, the public land still publicly owned. Whether it be in the stormy sting of winter, the sweet-scent of spring, the carefree embrace of summer, or the nostalgic and bittersweet dazzle of autumn, this place still inspires people to respect an entire creation that we could never, ever replace. Finally, this place reminds us that each generation has its obligations to the children of the future. One of those obligations is to treat the earth with wisdom and with care, and here in Oregon, the spirit of the land calls for nothing less.

IN AUTUMN, BIGLEAF MAPLE LEAVES FALL ALONG NORTH SILVER CREEK IN SILVER FALLS STATE PARK.

Aspen leaves turn brilliant at Shoalwater Bay in Upper Klamath Lake.

WIZARD ISLAND RISES OUT OF CRATER LAKE, WHERE OREGON CONSERVATIONISTS PROPOSE AN EXPANDED NATIONAL
PARK TO PROTECT THE GREATER ECOSYSTEM OF THIS UNIQUE AREA.

A RED OCTAGONAL BARN STANDS IN THE FOREGROUND OF THE WALLOWA MOUNTAINS.

THE NORTH FORK OF THE UMPQUA RIVER, ONE OF OREGON'S GREAT STEELHEAD STREAMS,
SHIMMERS PAST FIR TREES AND WESTERN DOGWOODS.

ABOVE: NATIVE BUNCHGRASSES AT THE ZUMWALT PRAIRIE PRESERVE GROW IN AN ABUNDANCE
NOW FOUND IN FEW OTHER PLACES OWING TO THE INVASION OF EXOTIC GRASSES AND WEEDS.

FACING PAGE: EAGLE CAP RISES OVER SUNSHINE LAKE IN THE EAGLE CAP
WILDERNESS, WALLOWA MOUNTAINS.

Above: The sun sets behind the Cape Meares Lighthouse in northern Oregon.

Right: Mount Hood—to many people a symbol of the Oregon landscape—
reflects with the last light of the day in the tranquil waters of Lost Lake.

The placid waters of Waldo Lake mark the source of the Willamette River.

CONSERVATION RESOURCES

1000 Friends of Oregon
534 SW 3rd Avenue, Suite 300
Portland, OR 97204
Phone: (503) 497-1000
Fax: (503) 223-0073
www.friends.org

Audubon Society of Portland
5151 NW Cornell Road
Portland, OR 97210
Phone: (503) 292-6855
Fax: (503) 292-1021
www.audubonportland.org

Cascadia Times
25-6 NW 23rd Place, #406
Portland, OR 97210
Phone: (503) 223-9036
www.times.org

Forest Service Employees
  for Environmental Ethics
P.O. Box 11615
Eugene, OR 97440
Phone: (541) 484-2692
Fax: (541) 484-3004
www.fseee.org

Friends of the Columbia Gorge
522 SW 5th Avenue, Suite 820
Portland, OR 97204
Phone: (503) 241-3762
Fax: (503) 241-3873
www.gorgefriends.org

Northwest Environmental Defense Center
10015 SW Terwilliger Boulevard
Portland, OR 97219
Phone: (503) 768-6673
Fax: (503) 768-6671
www.nedc.org

Oregon Environmental Council
520 SW 6th Avenue, Suite 940
Portland, OR 97204
Phone: (503) 222-1963
Fax: (503) 222-1405
www.orcouncil.org

Oregon Natural Desert Association
16 NW Kansas Avenue
Bend, OR 97701
Phone: (541) 330-2638
Fax: (541) 385-3370
www.onda.org

Oregon Trout
117 SW Naito Parkway
Portland, OR 97204
Phone: (503) 222-9091
www.ortrout.org

Pacific Rivers Council
P.O. Box 10798
Eugene, OR 97440
Phone: (541) 345-0119
Fax: (541) 345-0710
www.pacrivers.org

Save Our Wild Salmon Coalition
2031 SE Belmont Street
Portland, OR 97214
Phone: (503) 230-0421
Fax: (503) 230-0677
www.wildsalmon.org

Sierra Club, Oregon Chapter
2950 SE Stark Street, Suite 110
Portland, OR 97214
Phone: (503) 238-0442
Fax: (503) 238-6281
www.oregon.sierraclub.org

Siskiyou Project
P.O. Box 220
Cave Junction, OR 97523
Phone: (541) 592-4459
www.siskiyou.org

The Nature Conservancy of Oregon
821 SE 14th Avenue
Portland, OR 97214
Phone: (503) 230-1221
Fax: (503) 230-9639
www.tnc.org/oregon

Trout Unlimited
Western Conservation Office
213 SW Ash Street
Suite 205
Portland, OR 97204
Phone: (503) 827-5700
www.tu.org

WaterWatch of Oregon
213 SW Ash St., Suite 208
Portland, OR 97204
Phone: (503) 295-4039
Fax: (503) 295-2791
www.waterwatch.org

BIBLIOGRAPHY

Alt, David D., and Donald W. Hyndman. *Roadside Geology of Oregon*. Missoula, MT: Mountain Press Publishing, 1978.

Ashworth, William. *The Wallowas: Coming of Age in the Wilderness*. New York: Hawthorn Books, 1978.

Cone, Joseph. *A Common Fate: Endangered Salmon and the People of the Pacific Northwest*. New York: Henry Holt, 1995.

Cox, Thomas R. *The Park Builders: A History of State Parks in the Pacific Northwest*. Seattle: University of Washington Press, 1988.

Daniel, John. *The Trail Home: Nature, Imagination, and the American West*. New York: Pantheon Books, 1994.

Defenders of Wildlife and Oregon Biodiversity Project. *Oregon's Living Landscape: Strategies and Opportunities to Conserve Biodiversity*. Corvallis, OR: Oregon State University Press, 1998.

Durbin, Kathie. *Tree Huggers: Victory, Defeat & Renewal in the Northwest Ancient Forest Campaign*. Seattle: The Mountaineers Books, 1996.

Kirk, Ruth, ed. *The Enduring Forests: Northern California, Oregon, Washington, British Columbia, and Southeast Alaska*. Seattle: The Mountaineers Books, 1996.

Koberstein, Paul, ed. *Cascadia Times*, quarterly newspaper published in Portland, 1995–2003.

Komar, Paul D. *The Pacific Northwest Coast: Living with the Shores of Oregon and Washington*. Durham, NC: Duke University Press, 1998.

Langston, Nancy. *Forest Dreams, Forest Nightmares: The Paradox of Old Growth in the Inland West*. Seattle: University of Washington Press, 1995.

LaRoe, Edward T., et al. *Our Living Resources: A Report to the Nation on the Distribution, Abundance, and Health of U.S. Plants, Animals, and Ecosystems*. Washington, D.C.: U.S. Department of the Interior, National Biological Service, 1995.

Loy, William G., Stuart Allan, Aileen R. Buckley, and James E. Meacham. *Atlas of Oregon*. Corvallis, OR: University of Oregon Press, 2001.

Luoma, Jon R. *The Hidden Forest: The Biography of an Ecosystem*. New York: Henry Holt, 1999.

Mathews, Daniel. *Cascade-Olympic Natural History*. Portland: Raven Editions and Portland Audubon Society, 1988.

Norse, Elliott A. *Ancient Forests of the Pacific Northwest*. Washington, D.C.: Island Press, 1990.

Olson, Larry N., and John Daniel. *Oregon Rivers*. Englewood, CO: Westcliffe Publishers, 1997.

Peirce, Neal R. *The Pacific States of America: People, Politics, and Power in the Five Pacific Basin States*. New York: W. W. Norton, 1972.

Palmer, Tim. *America by Rivers*. Washington, D.C.: Island Press, 1996.

Palmer, Tim. *The Columbia: Sustaining a Modern Resource*. Seattle: The Mountaineers Books, 1997.

Palmer, Tim. *Pacific High: Adventures in the Coast Ranges from Baja to Alaska*. Washington, D.C.: Island Press, 2002.

Palmer, Tim. *The Snake River: Window to the West*. Washington, D.C.: Island Press, 1991.

Palmer, Tim. *The Wild and Scenic Rivers of America*. Washington, D.C.: Island Press, 1993.

Pojar, Jim and Andy MacKinnon. *Plants of the Pacific Northwest Coast: Washington, Oregon, British Columbia, and Alaska*. Redmond, WA: Lone Pine Publishing, 1994.

Ricketts, Taylor H., et al. *Terrestrial Ecoregions of North America: A Conservation Assessment*. Washington, D.C.: Island Press, 1999.

Risser, Paul G. *Oregon State of the Environment Report*. Salem, OR: Oregon Progress Board, 2000.

Ryan, John C. *State of the Northwest*. Seattle: Northwest Environment Watch, 1994.

Schoonmaker, Peter K, et al. *The Rainforests of Home*. Washington, D.C.: Island Press, 1997.

Schultz, Stewart T. *The Northwest Coast: A Natural History*. Portland: Timber Press, 1990.

Seideman, David. *Showdown at Opal Creek: The Battle for America's Last Wilderness*. New York: Carroll & Graf Publishers, 1993.

Sullivan, William L. *Exploring Oregon's Wild Areas: A Guide for Hikers, Backpackers, Climbers, Cross-Country Skiers, Paddlers*, 3rd ed. Seattle: The Mountaineers Books, 2002.

Walth, Brent. *Fire at Eden's Gate: Tom McCall and the Oregon Story*. Portland: Oregon Historical Society Press, 1994.

Willamette Kayak and Canoe Club. *Soggy Sneakers: Guide to Oregon Rivers*. Corvallis, OR: Willamette Kayak and Canoe Club, 1986.

Wood, Wendell. *Oregon's Ancient Forests*. Portland: Oregon Natural Resources Council, 1991.

INDEX